Choruses and Counter-Choruses

Critical South

The publication of this series is supported by the International Consortium of Critical Theory Programs funded by the Andrew W. Mellon Foundation.

Mário Pinto de Andrade, *The Revolution Will Be a Poetic Act*
Leonor Arfuch, *Memory and Autobiography*
Hélé Béji, *We, the Decolonized*
Maurits van Bever Donker, *Texturing Difference*
Paula Biglieri and Luciana Cadahia, *Seven Essays on Populism*
Antônio Bispo dos Santos, *The Earth Gives, the Earth Wants*
Sueli Carneiro, *Dispositif of Raciality*
Gisela Catanzaro, *Spectrology of Authoritarian Neoliberalism*
Aimé Césaire, *Resolutely Black*
Aimé Césaire, *Toussaint Louverture*
Victoria J. Collis-Buthelezi and Aaron Kamugisha (eds.), *The Caribbean Race Reader*
Bolívar Echeverría, *Modernity and "Whiteness"*
Diego Falconí Trávez, *From Ashes to Text*
Celso Furtado, *The Myth of Economic Development*
Eduardo Grüner, *The Haitian Revolution*
Francisco-J. Hernández Adrián, *On Tropical Grounds*
Ailton Krenak, *Ancestral Future*
Ailton Krenak, *Life Is Not Useful*
Premesh Lalu, *Undoing Apartheid*
Karima Lazali, *Colonial Trauma*
María Pia López, *Not One Less*
Achille Mbembe and Felwine Sarr (eds.), *The Politics of Time*
Achille Mbembe and Felwine Sarr (eds.), *To Write the Africa World*
Valentin-Yves Mudimbe, *The Scent of the Father*
Pablo Oyarzun, *Doing Justice*
Néstor Perlongher, *Plebeian Prose*
Bento Prado Jr., *Error, Illusion, Madness*
Nelly Richard, *Eruptions of Memory*
Silvia Rivera Cusicanqui, *Ch'ixinakax utxiwa*
Suely Rolnik, *Spheres of Insurrection*
Rita Segato, *The War Against Women*
Tendayi Sithole, *The Black Register*
Maboula Soumahoro, *Black Is the Journey, Africana the Name*
Fatou Sow, *Feminism in Africa*
Flora Süssekind, *Choruses and Counter-Choruses*
Javad Tabatabai, *Ibn Khaldun and the Social Sciences*
Dénètem Touam Bona, *Fugitive, Where Are You Running?*

Choruses and Counter-Choruses

Culture and Politics in Brazil, 2013–2023

Flora Süssekind

Translated by Sergio Delgado Moya

polity

This edition is based on a revised version of a book titled *Coros, Contrários, Massa*, originally published in Portuguese by Cepe Editora in 2022.

Polity Press
65 Bridge Street
Cambridge CB2 1UR, UK

Polity Press
111 River Street
Hoboken, NJ 07030, USA

ISBN-13: 978-1-5095-6818-5 – hardback
ISBN-13: 978-1-5095-6819-2 – paperback

A catalogue record for this book is available from the British Library.

Library of Congress Control Number: 2026937190

Typeset in 10.5 on 12pt Sabon
by Fakenham Prepress Solutions, Fakenham, Norfolk NR21 8NL
Printed and bound in Great Britain by Ashford Colour Ltd.

For further information on Polity, visit our website:
politybooks.com

Contents

Figures

1

Regarding the Chorus

"What is left of the chorus, once the chorus is no longer there?": this question, borrowed from Martin Mégevand,[1] haunts every contemporary study of active choralities – not just as they appear on stage, in the sphere of theater, but also as they emerge in other discursive fields and in different artistic practices. Chorality is a term first disseminated by theater analyst Jean-Pierre Sarrazac. Conceived as a particular and plural tendency; as a polyphony that is not to be confused with "the principles of dialogism";[2] as something constituted, first and foremost, by paratactic dispersion, by interweaving; and by the constant tension produced by opposing forces – chorality suggests, as Mégevand writes, something beyond "the history of the arts of spectacle," a crossway of several disciplines and different art forms.

The study of this crossway demands an engagement with extant writings on the common and the communal, specifically with the works of Maurice Blanchot (*The Unavowable Community*) and Jean-Luc Nancy (*The Compearance*, *The Inoperative Community*, *The Disavowed Community*). Choralities that break through when the chorus is no longer present ground their composition precisely on the knowledge that the notion of the common cannot be fully expressed, and neither can the sense of the radically heterogeneous that this notion evokes and desires. In this sense, and as Christopher Triau suggests, the emergence of multiple forms of chorality does not presuppose the existence of a community; on the contrary, it involves the constant probing of the notion of community, perpetually working at its limits.[3]

That same, constant work, at the limits of the notion of community, may well be the function behind the intensification of choral irruptions witnessed in a country like Brazil, which has seen, in recent years – particularly since the so-called *Jornadas de Junho* in 2013 and, after that, since the impeachment of Dilma Rousseff initiated in 2015 – the splintering of the social pact formulated in the Constitution of 1988. At the same time, awareness of the fragile underpinnings of a minimally democratic shared existence has been expanding (in the context of both growing intolerance and the increasing presence of neofascist ideologies and active groups).

With this in mind, it is worth recalling Antônio Cândido's *On Literature and Society*, and his three studies of naturalist novels where the author brings together contrasting, spatialized representations of the collective as they appear in three works of nineteenth-century literature: Zola's *L'Assommoir* (1877); Giovanni Verga's *I Malavoglia* (1881); and Aluísio Azevedo's *O Cortiço* (1890). In this comparative work, and particularly in reference to the Brazilian novel, Cândido reaches the following conclusion. If, in *L'Assommoir*, "the story of Gervaise leads us directly to the mental experience of poverty," in *O Cortiço*, on the contrary, "between the concrete, particular representation (the *cortiço*) and our perception of poverty Brazil stands as an intermediary." This is because, as Cândido underlines, "there was such need for national self-definition, that writers seemed to have been constrained if they did use discourse to represent the nation with every step they took."[4]

In contemporary forms of chorality (which, due to the nature of their movement, escape from any kind of territorialization), there erupts, all the time and almost inevitably, a sense of the nation. In most instances, however, when the image of the nation irrupts in works of Brazilian arts and culture produced in the last decade, it does so in a splintered and mournful way. And it does, most importantly, as a kind of rumor. Voices, screams, honks, city noises, and gunshots are what sometimes brings to the scene this image of the nation. Other times, it is watchwords, singing, the sound of steps and car chases, the sounds of dance. Three recent films, all of them beautiful experiments in choralization, capture this form of irruption: Maria Augusta Ramos' O *processo* (2018), Eryk Rocha's *Cinema novo* (2016), and Eliane Caffé's *Era o Hotel Cambridge* (2016).

Ramos' film investigates Dilma Rousseff's impeachment process. It features an explicitly documentary plot line that concludes with Rousseff's removal from office, and it also imposes, from the very beginning, another plot line: a soundtrack that follows (sometimes loudly, at other times almost mutely) the commanding, factual register of the film. Those who watch the film can thus hear not just recorded testimony related to the impeachment (as well as individual responses and public conversations related to the same process), but also, and crucially, the indistinct and uninterrupted murmur of voices in the halls of Congress. The film also layers, as part of its soundtrack, the choral division between anti-democratic groups and groups assembled to resist the 2016 coup against Rousseff. As the film goes on, another layer of sound enters its sonic space: exploding tear gas canisters, gun shots, screams, and the sound of people running away from violence, all of which collectively prefigures the militarization of the country's administration that would, in fact, take place in 2018, and during Bolsonaro's government. Toward the beginning, the film features a clear view of the buildings in the city, as well as of people going about their day as residents and workers in the Brazilian capital. As it draws to an end, though, and in consonance with the soundtrack of the film, the ambient sound of the film becomes more and more anonymous, and the visual landscape, in turn, disappears behind a thick, dark fog of tear gas.

In *Cinema novo*, Eryk Rocha works with two broad lines of choralization: the sight and sound of several voices on screen speaking about *cinema novo*, and a remixing of visual and sonic fragments from archival sources (from films and from interviews with the filmmakers who defined that period in the history of Brazilian cinema). As the film goes on, these two lines of choralization eventually unfold into several series (scenes of people running, love scenes, a series on bodies, a series on struggle, and so forth) constructed through montage and by means of the overlays that the film eventually composes.

There are moments in the film where the image on screen and the sound extracted from archival sources stand in nonsynchronous relation to each other; these moments suggest, within the context of each series, possibilities of rupture and recombination that result in new choral splinterings. This, in turn, also highlights the strategic heterochrony of the film. The different registers that appear on screen do so in a fragmentary way, and they become present in a context different from their context of production. They're invoked with a sense of urgency, demarcating, nonetheless, the historical alterity that separates the referenced fragments from the context in which they're called into presence. The film also opens, at the same time, a field of mutual resonance between these different registers and their respective contexts.

Era o Hotel Cambridge – like Antônio Cândido's triptych of essays – centers on a spatialized, collective character: a building, which the film uses to reveal, from within, the struggle for the right to housing in Brazil. Deliberately, the film draws viewers into a kind of careful listening, starting with the sounds of the city and then moving on to the individualized sounds of a building (the creaks, the sound of dripping water, the banging of pipes, the thud and thump of steps). The building featured in the film is occupied by unhoused workers, refugees, migrants, and families. This is a building that operates like a loud, continuous chorality, and though the film isolates a few individual voices from that chorality, the building and the chorality it embodies act collectively: in assemblies, in the staging of group *tableaux vivants*, in building projects, in other actions taken by the occupants of the building, and in their confrontation with (and escape from) the police.

The list of choral forms present in the film is vast. They range from the elated song that rises up the staircase as the new occupants enter the building, to the choreographed movements made in semi-darkness, down to the changing rhythms and intensities of the vocal exchanges that take place within this space. One of the occupants (Carmen Silva Ferreira) takes on the role of corypheus, and some others appear as more or less individualized characters. Overall, though, what the film frames is a chorus of diverse languages, nationalities, trades, and professions. The film underlines this diversity while it points to the common but provisional space that emerges both from the shared occupancy of the building and from the forms of joint political action undertaken by the occupants.

As it winds down, the film sheds light on police efforts to regain control of the building and to disperse its current occupants, and in so doing it draws attention both to the limits and the vulnerabilities of occupations (in their current iteration), and to the significance of occupations in terms of communization and transformation of the urban experience. This draws the film and the perspective the film offers to reflections such as those provided by André Lepecki in *Exhausting Dance: Performance and the Politics of Movement*, by Andrew Hewitt in *Social Choreography*, and by Randy Martin in *Critical Moves*, all of whom produce approximations to the idea of choreography as political practice and as a register (in movement) of urban settings that make space for contestation. It's worth recalling, in that sense, Lepecki's remarks on the act of occupying, on the occupation: "refusing circulation, a still act takes on political, cinematic, and aesthetic aspects, for occupation and standing still demonstrate and reveal how impetus and the imperative of circulation and agitation are choreographies that police, block, and impede another, different vision of life."[5]

In Eliane Caffé's film, social choreography is evoked by a chorus of occupants that appears on screen talking and singing and dancing, a chorus that moves all the time, though not in accordance with the eviction notice enforced by the police. The sense of refusal here, of revolt, is highlighted by a comment made by Carmen Silva Ferreira, featured and doubly framed in the film (Ferreira delivers her message through a computer image shown on screen). Suggestively, Ferreira's remarks help viewers identify moments where the film bridges the gap between contemporary choralities, on the one hand, and the political dimension of choruses in ancient Greece. The speech made by the corypheus-leader of the occupation, as she faces the threatening arrival of police at the building and their calls to vacate it, is one such moment. Our order, the corypheus states, will be a total disordering of the system. And the disorder of the system is our order.

In this sense, it's helpful to point out how Nicole Loraux's book *La Voix endeuillée* complicates the work accomplished by Mégevand on the choral formations that are made possible by the present moment. Loraux's book brings together a series of essays on Greek tragedy, and it begins with a critique of Sartre's adaptation of *The Trojan Women* by Euripides, where the French author does away with the choral laments present in the original version, transforming them into dialogue.

Loraux questions this decision by Sartre, who does away with the oracle structure of the play on the grounds that it was not dramatic enough, that it was incapable of conveying a sense of struggle. She argues, instead, after analyzing the possible resonances of Greek tragedy in our present circumstances, that it is precisely in the lyrical and dialogic segments of the choral laments – in their oratory nature, in their literal materiality, in their tone and metric structure, in their very distribution – that Euripides' tragedy is potentialized in the present.[6]

What Loraux argues is that our "sense of proximity," our engagement with the meaning of the tragic, takes place precisely through the act of listening to that voice of mourning, and in the act of comprehending the conflictive matter at the heart of that lament (the same matter Sartre was unable, or unwilling, to grasp). Conflict, in the sense Loraux alludes to here – and synthesizing her own words – can be said to be different from the act of placing themes or contents in a relationship of opposition; rather, conflict in this sense is constituted by the elements that materially constitute tragedy as a dramaturgical form and as meaningful discourse.[7] As Loraux points out, conflict also includes everything that opposes direct political references and strictly anti-political behavior, everything that resists the strangling forces of the polis, everything that stands against prescriptive amnesia. It includes, in short, the kind of mourning that, on the contrary, revives and activates the potency of memory.

The background invoked by Loraux for her scholarship on tragedy is the amnesty extended in 1972 to the French Nazi collaborator Paul Touvier,[8] as well as the publication of the 1978 interview with the former Commissioner-General for Jewish Affairs under the Vichy Régime, Louis Darquier de Pellepoix.[9] As Loraux puts it,[10] her writings on tragedy work against these efforts, pointing, instead, toward the need for remembrance, the necessity of keeping alive the memories of past calamities.

Toward the end of *La Voix endeuillée*, Loraux reiterates that her essay on tragedy and on the essential place of the chorus aspires, most of all, to both highlight the memory of pain, and create conditions that allow one to listen to "the mournful voice of tragedy." In so doing, it also aspires to redefine the choruses' political dimension, by drawing attention to the very materiality of the chorus' words, rhythms, songs, and movements, and by proposing an understanding of the force of chorality that goes far beyond the habitual insistence on its civic dimension, and that emphasizes, on the contrary, its resistance to the orders of the polis.

Let us keep this in mind, and return now to the rumor, the chatter, the voices, and the dispersed sounds that run through – and at times overflow – all three films discussed earlier in this speculation concerning the chorus. Let us also consider the clash or resonance that takes place between the different elements, voices, and materials convened in the choralities analyzed throughout the course of this book. A sense of friction is present in both instances, an almost audible disjunction, a tension that persists beyond the experience sustained by these works. It operates as an enduring lament whose disharmonious force manages to remain active. The act of listening to those choruses is the subject matter and the analytical method of the following essays, all of which are moved by an urgent desire to be in dialogue with the present moment.

The fundamental objective at the heart of these reflections is the construction of an analytic field guided by a reading of historical contexts where choralities are activated and reconfigured – a reading, furthermore, that wishes to highlight the difference between these contexts. The analytic field I strive to construct is shaped by a careful consideration of polyphonic and intermedia methods that emerge from the study of the composition of particular artistic and literary works (and also from some collective movements) being observed here. It is also shaped by the conceptual substrates I bring to these essays, substrates that stem from my work in theater, literary, and aesthetic studies, which seek to resonate in the sphere of the social sciences. This last point is important, because the political dimension of choruses becomes manifest in their plural aspect, and because the superimposing of languages and materialities that operates in them gets intensified when discord and dynamic conflict (as opposed to conjugation and consensus) are embraced as constitutive elements that need to be understood and activated.

The focus of this book, then, falls on choruses that don't necessarily emerge from the world of theater, or from the realm of the epic. It falls, rather, on choralities that arise as structuring or destabilizing forces operating in artistic and cultural practices, and in historically specific circumstances. Most relevant to me was the desire to observe them in a very specific historical context – the recent social and political juncture in Brazil – all the while making room for retrospective interaction with previous practices and previous moments. Along the way, the book leaves behind a register constructed by means of choralizations: a register of transformations and of the more emphatic politicization of forms of cultural intervention conceived and deployed in response to the expansive, conservative assault Brazil has experienced during the last decade.

There is more than one reason why the chorus, as a character with some kind of wide collective appeal, seems unviable in Brazil in the present moment. Chief among them is the fraying of the social pact that undergirded the "New Republic," as well as the increasing difficulty of projecting an imagined community at a national scale. The same reasons that make the chorus unviable as a character, however, also seem, paradoxically, to intensify choral irruptions of varying scales and in various media. Because of the very otherness of their chorality, these irruptions, in turn, evoke the double absence of both the chorus and the common, the same absence we touched upon when considering the work of Mégevand. In one and the same movement, they point to the living matter – the internal discord – that defines them and that also signals their refusal of unison, homogeneity, and generalization (all of which are usually, and rather reductively, associated with choral configurations).

At this juncture, it is worth highlighting choral formations that are structured by dispute, as is the case of poetry slams, an artistic and cultural practice that has been growing in Brazil in the last few decades. The conflictual nature of poetry slams becomes especially evident when slams are held in open public spaces. There, the relationship between the social critique vocalized by slammers, on the one hand, and the impact of their spoken-word poetry on a captive or passing public, on the other hand, becomes more accentuated. The sense of citizenship of anonymous spectators who stop to experience a poetry slam is amplified by this very experience. The act of concurring with the critiques and the experiences voiced by the poets, the act of taking a stance vis-à-vis the issues articulated by their words, politically rescales spectators who take part in this form of collective listening, and who thus become an active part of what is often an abrupt or unexpected communal configuration.

Other choral forms, some of which enjoy strong popular backing in Brazil, also come to mind: samba schools, those immense choruses that contend with each other during Carnival; the more informal and disordered *blocos* organized during the same festivities; the various kinds of processions, rituals, and regular street festivities or encounters that occur all year long (from *via crucis* to *bumba meu boi*, from *fogueteiros* to *rodas de samba*). Sporting events also come to mind here, as discussed in Hans Ulrich Gumbrecht's observations regarding both soccer games (and soccer fans, or *torcidas*) in Brazil and the formation of a communal body at these events, as well as the link between these huge communal bodies of fans and the notion of the mystical body of Christ as conceived and practiced by the Catholic Church.

Sporting events, of course, can also result in group convergences that can suddenly turn violent, the kind of convergences that assault rival sporting fans and individuals who, for whatever reason, become targets of aggression. In this sense, sporting events can start to look like the lynchings that were so frequent in Brazil and elsewhere in decades past, and that are always threatening to come back (and not just in the digital world) – the same lynchings that I analyze briefly in this book, in dialogue with the work of José de Souza Martins and in reference to the literary works of Veronica Stigger.

In direct contrast to this form of violence (sudden and unwarranted as it so often seems to be), and as an example of collective and organized responses to structural social exclusions, this book also grapples with occupations of urban spaces. As a result of the diversity of their participants, and due to their constitutive identitarian, linguistic, and religious plurality, these occupations take on a manifestly choral configuration. They stand among the most significant examples of this form of configuration, in terms of their diversity, their political reach, and some effective anti-totalitarian actions.

Occupations took place during the 2013 *Jornadas de Junho*,[11] but during and after the 2016 coup against Dilma Rousseff they multiplied extensively. Consider, for instance, the occupations of institutes by public high school students all over the nation and, also, the so-called "Ocupa Minc," the 70-day long occupation of the Gustavo Capanema Palace (the former headquarters of Brazil's Ministry of Education and Health) in Rio de Janeiro, a protest organized against the government of Michel Temer and, in particular, against the efforts to extinguish the Ministry of Culture. Consider, too, the occupations of abandoned buildings by movements of *sem-teto* in urban centers, as portrayed in

Eliane Caffé's previously mentioned film. All these different occupations had massive political impact and were some of the most efficient and denunciatory resistance strategies organized in the face of the 2016 coup.

These massive and more visible choral configurations, the ones with the most social impact, are not, however, my main object of interest. Their echoes are perceptible, even silently, in all the chapters. But what I'm really after here are the choruses that emerge beyond the main stage, so to speak: the experiments that work eventually or methodically, insidiously or loudly, as sites and procedures of transformation and variation. What I'm after are non-canonical choralities that cross artistic and discursive divides, choralities that broach the line between a field and what's beyond a field, choralities whose force of displacement and force of contrast have the capacity to redefine the contours of a field. What I'm after, in short, are choralities capable of composing a register of movements and clashes – choralities that can also, in this process, affect and rethink their own rhythmic and speculative configuration.

This book will explore a few hypotheses that circumscribe some kinds of choral formations within specific conceptual frameworks (the grammar of the middle class, for instance, as evoked in the work of Vilma Arêas, Veronica Stigger, and André Sant'Anna). The singularity and the interrelationship of specific artistic and literary methods will be, however, the sites where I'll seek lines of conjunction and variation – the sites where I'll analyze, in their affinities and their differences, some of the peculiar manifestations of the clearly choral inflection embodied in contemporary cultural production. In this regard, a few experiments stand out as particularly elucidating. Among them are works by Augusto de Campos, André Vallias, Nuno Ramos, Bia Lessa, Lenora de Barros, and Ricardo Aleixo, works where constitutive polyphony stands alongside material and expressive reconfigurations. Also elucidating is the trajectory of someone like the poet Carlito Azevedo, whose exercises in the theatricalization of poetry have been subjecting diction itself, rhythmically reinventing poems in the different arrangements afforded by serialization ("As banhistas"), montage (*Livro das postagens*), and vocalization.

The study of each artist's work is here done comparatively, through a series of contrasting approaches. These are the concepts and themes that analytically circumscribe the studies brought together in this book: (1) the forms of enunciative tension that shape and bring conflict to the compositional experiments here convened; (2) the use of specific procedures and the internal variation of these procedures; (3) the processes of fabulation and structuring that unfold in these experiments, through reframing (Vilma Arêas, Giselle Beiguelman), ventriloquizing (André Sant'Anna, Noemi Jaffe, Nuno Ramos, Grace Passô), and differential coupling (as seen in the series of duplicated structures that I offer as counterpoints to a parasitic technopolitics, in the last essay of this book).

My intent, then, is to contrast these lines of inquiry and my commentary on individual artistic trajectories with both wider historical frameworks, and also to a critical reconfiguration of the operational-theoretical field to which these choral irruptions belong – a field that exceeds strict domains, to the extent that these irruptions are both discordant and complementary, and inasmuch as this feature troubles any kind of formatting or classification attempt. The choral irruptions here analyzed migrate between different languages, media, and fields of activity, and in that sense, in that performative movement, they demand a non-consensual reason, as well as a critical perspective that perhaps could be best described as choreographic, or, better – rhythmical.

2

Dissonant Choralities (and the Context of the 2013 *Jornadas de Junho*)

By the time the *Jornadas de Junho*[1] emerged in Brazil in 2013, before a wave of protests gripped the nation that same year, a significant number of texts had already pushed choral experiences to the foreground. These experiences, as featured in these texts, are marked by acts of listening, and by the construction of a kind of echo chamber, where rumors – those whispers that sound, at first, unclassifiable, simultaneous – multiply their reverberations: the rumor of a multiplicity of voices, of nonverbal elements, of overlapping registers and diverse, intersecting modes of expression.

There's an intentional tension in these choralities: a tension between genres, repertoires, and categories that are usually fundamental for the constitution of a literary sphere. This tension, in turn, transforms intersecting noises and sounds that are seemingly unintelligible into a form of interrogation of both the historical moment and the literary field. The fact that these sounds and noises link this field to other areas of cultural production (film, for instance) is not coincidental. This audibility is evinced, for example, by the strong presence of the sonic world in two films from the beginning of the 2000s, two films that are paradoxically at odds with each other: one of them is an exercise in listening to the city; the other is attuned to the sound of silence. What I have in mind is, of course, Kleber Mendonça Filho's *Neigboring Sounds* (*O Som ao Redor*, 2012) and Cao Guimarães' *The Soul of the Bone* (*A Alma do Osso*, 2004). This tense soundscape can be perceived in other areas of cultural production, and is particularly manifest in the work of certain collectives and art groups, such as Chelpa Ferro and its experiments with sonic art. Most tellingly, it is also at the heart of the reinvention of the chorus in Brazilian theater productions of the last decade, as witnessed in the trajectory of José Celso Martinez Corrêa and his Teatro Oficina Uzyna Uzona. His works feature the function of choruses in protagonist roles, in constant variations.

"In this egoistic, competitive millennium, at the end of neoliberalism," it is "an immense task to rediscover that initial choral matter,"[2] emphasizes José Celso. Alongside the emphasis on diverse forms of chorality by the Uzyna Uzona group, one can add the continued action of groups such as Grupo XIX de Teatro and the Teatro da Vertigem, not only in the sense of collective processes of scenic-dramaturgical creation, but also in their research into the operations of specific choral performances. It is possible to add to these examples an experiment in theatrical audibility such as *Labirinto*, staged by Moacir Chaves and Alfândega 88 Group, using two texts by the rarely staged nineteenth-century Brazilian author Qorpo Santo.

We can also connect this rediscovery of the artistic and political possibilities of "choral matter" to the modes of association, mutual interference, and exchange of experiences among some companies and collectives. This was the case of the "Coletivo Improviso," which acted as a kind of collective (and public) dialogue between multidisciplinary artists who created together scenes, images, choreographies, texts, and videos through improvisation. Together, they occupied, during these artistic actions, different, previously chosen urban areas. Enrique Diaz, Mariana Lima, Denise Stutz, Gustavo Ciríaco, Renato Linhares, Daniela Amorim, among other musicians, dancers, performers from various fields, each with independent trajectories, periodically reunited to share their research and to experiment together with different scenic and intervention possibilities, always emphasizing invention and improvisation. Their actions were frequently linked to different dialogues with urban space, sometimes involving brief interventions in pre-defined locations that were temporarily transformed during their occupation, as in "Não olhe agora" ("Don't Look Now").[3]

And there are also singular actions, such as those convened by Patrick Sampaio, for example (some very brief, in various locations in Rio de Janeiro).

I don't mean to suggest that there are no other irruptions of choral modes in Brazilian literary culture. They happen frequently, and they're usually linked to processes of removal or to disruptions of form, of artistic media, of dominant textual models, and destabilizations of the cultural field at large. One example of dynamic disruption of form – of diction, of the compositional structure of a narrative poem – is the theatricalization that takes place within *O guesa*, by Joachim Sousândrade, specially in Cantos II and X. There is a sonic thickening in it so dense that it renders impossible any ideal of univocality or any epic control of the poem. Genres, voices, languages, geographies interact within a disruptive mode that affects not only Sousândrade's writing but Brazilian romanticism as well.

Other examples of choral disruption, this time from the modernist period, could include the cut-up voices and pieces of appropriated works found in Oswald de Andrade´s writings, in the collage composition method he used in *O homem e o cavalo*, for example, and in the satirical refigurations of the memoir he produced between 1920 and 1930, a defining moment for Brazilian literary practice. In close critical dialogue with modernism, the 1960s tropicalist moment can also be seen as a vast choral intervention, to the extent that it constituted both an interartistic exchange and a series of collective operations.

We can think, additionally and in the same vein, of the choral dimension of some poetic methods, like the initial, collective assertion of the concrete poetry project in Brazil and its triple, verbivocovisual orientation (verbal, vocal, and visual). Examples include the polymorphous voices – and the radically hurried speech – that make a significant portion of Chico Alvim's poetry a perverse choral composition. Or the way the poem materializes in diverse media and in different materialities in Augusto de Campos' poetic method, as well as in the increasing internal theatrical unfolding (dramatic monologues, dialogues, addressing modes) that takes place in the poetry of Carlito Azevedo, especially after his *Versos de circunstância*.

Several texts published during the first decades of the twenty-first century in Brazil carry a strong choral logic into contemporary literary culture. In more radical experiments, their reception could be described using the expression disseminated by Christophe Hanna – "unidentifed verbal objects,"[4] or UVOs. Hanna playfully reworks the term UFO to discuss processes, contexts, and the critical function of certain literary experiments that can come across as elusive or hard to classify. What makes these experiments categorically unrecognizable is, most of all, the fact that, unfortunately, their (literary) field of insertion reinforces not speculation but classification. This field is guided by institutional devices (normativities) and conceptual or interpretive axes (the ones that privilege homogenization, stability, and controlled expansion) – devices and axes that the experiments mentioned above knowingly brush aside.

The dislocations operating in choral dissensual forms contrast with the preference for identity and the identifiable cultivated by controlled, stabilizing, homogenizing cultural devices. Examples of recent enactments of these conflictive choralities can be found in the latest productions by André Sant'Anna (even in his minimalist monologues, such as the satirically titled "Commentary, Online, About Everything That's Happening Out There,"[5] published in *Folha de São Paulo* on June 20, 2010), in Antonio Geraldo Figueiredo Ferreira's narrative *As visitas que hoje estamos* (2012), in Veronica Stigger's work (specially her *Delírio de damasco*, 2012), and in Beatriz Bracher's fiction (particularly *I Didn't Talk*, 2017; *Antonio*, 2007; and "Cloc, clac," included in *meu amor*, 2009). Another example of these enactments is also found in Teixera Coelho's *História natural da ditadura* (2006), a book that, strangely enough, has not been widely read, and that is constituted by the comparative unfolding of states of exception and the internal echoes of different historical authoritarian moments.

These works share a sense of kinship in their use of destabilizing choral procedures, like in the narrative works by Lourenço Mutarelli that function on a double register, verbal and visual. And like *A arte de produzir efeito sem causa*, where graphic incursions make this twofold function evident, and *O natimorto*, where the visual dimension is brought into the narrative by a character who interprets the ghastly photographs that illustrate health warnings on cigarette packs. They're also close to Marília Garcia's *Engano geográfico* (2012), with its methodic fluctuation of voices arranged between mistakes (geographical ones, as the title of the book suggests) and a profound sense of the haphazard. And then, of course, there is the work of Nuno Ramos. Beyond the structural fold – between narration and meditation – at the heart of *Ó* (2008), one of the most important prose experiments in recent Brazilian literature, we also have his whole series of "Falas," some of which are explicitly choral compositions that are often included (sometimes as acousmatic voices) in his visual–acoustic installations.

It is curious to observe, amidst these verbal experiments, how most commentaries on current Brazilian literary production are dominated by an evident resistance to questioning poetics "incapable of understanding the radically new."[6] It's worth, then, dwelling for a moment on some critical reviews published in the cultural pages of *O Globo* newspaper.

In one such review, "Viver de literatura" ("Living from Literature"), signed by Luiz Ruffato,[7] the critic comes out in defense of the professionalization of the writer and the expansion of the Brazilian literary market. Praiseful in his assessment of the place of professionalized writers, Ruffato falls short, on the other hand, of pointing out what this "place" is and what it means to occupy it. Ruffato's defense of professionalized writing does not seem concerned with the broader discussion of what makes possible this kind of (professionalized) writerly intervention, nor does it seem concerned with questioning what constitutes a "successful" work (the kind whose themes and topics are self-justified and capable of earning the author a living). Nowhere in this defense of the professionalized writer do we find a willingness to interrogate textual models amenable to easy and unproblematic redeployment, the kind that seems to inform how likely a writer is to hold on to a contract with a large publishing house and a place in the global book market. Small wonder, then, that some writers who showed early promise in their ability to question current standards of interference and intelligibility seem to quickly lose their sense of vigor and insubordination to the laws of the market, of trending topics, of easy applause.

It's just as curious to witness, in a book by Regina Dalcastagnè,[8] the veiled resurrection of "literature as mimetic representation," a revival buttressed both by fin-de-siècle notions of unified perspective and literary genre, and by an unambiguous and uncomplicated understanding of what literature is (affirmative, homogenizing territory, marked by thematic readings and identitarian convergences of nation, gender, and class). Choral forms, on the other hand, present a problem for these acts of critical classification, immediate as they are and entirely lacking in judgment ("classification" in this sense dispenses with analysis and leaves the little storage boxes of critique entirely unaltered). Choral works are often intentionally difficult to focus on; they involve multiple forms of material refiguration (not to be confused with simple adaptation) and they deliberately suspend mechanical formalization. They thus implode restrictive approaches to literature that seem unwilling or incapable of going beyond systemic binary oppositions that insist on pitting fiction against testimony, sequentiality against fragmentation, constructiveness against expressiveness, and so forth.

Leyla Perrone-Moisés' "A literatura exigente"[9] ("Demanding Literature"), another evaluation of contemporary Brazilian literature published in *O Globo*, packs more weight in its observations. It brings into focus cracks in the literary field, but the sides in this field defined by the article (the sides that end up on either side of these cracks) get reduced to little more than contrasting elements: a simple opposition between a literature of entertainment and a demanding kind of literature. In this view, the "demanding" in demanding literature is filtered through the lens of thematic and stylistic generalizations (mistrust, half-spoken words, residues, the absence of the father), generalizations that manage to cluster together very different cultural attitudes.

There are, of course, works that are more than demanding, and there's no comparison between, on the one hand, these (purposedly opaque) literary works and the writers for whom each process of formalization is equally problematic and, on the other hand, authors who falsely believe that experimentation is nothing more than a kind of literary prêt-à-porter, involving techniques that have been long assimilated, ready-made. These are the writers who are mainly interested in becoming a successful "medalhão," to use the expression coined in 1881 by Machado de Assis to describe the non-radicality, the superficial cultural knowledge and literary work, that usually is key to academic recognition and popular appeal in Brazilian literary life.

A merit of Perrone's analysis is the importance she attributes to writers who make an effort to move beyond market logics and the logic of literature as entertainment. We should note, furthermore, that even in the face of this logic, and in reference to writers beyond the purview of Perrone's analysis, consequential destabilizations that have not been neutralized are still visible, and they stand in contrast to the attempts to resume and re-institutionalize regressive lines of continuity in Brazilian literary culture (among them: simplistic naturalisms, emphatic testimonies, taxonomic inventories, customs and manners, and the poem as pre-defined technique). Curiously enough, these attempts gained momentum around the same time that a drive to re-democratize the country was taking shape in the political sphere. What can surely be ascertained, nonetheless, is an ongoing process of increased complexity in literary production – a process that perhaps has not been matched by a critical and conceptual response as vigorous as this literary production demands.

The lack of an adequate critical response could well be the reason why several of these works make apparent, from the outset, their resistance to formal interpretations that trade in immediacy or lack of mediation. Now let's take a closer look at some of the books that did not receive a real critical response and were thrown, instead, into the storage bin of unindentified literary objects. Most of them are very diverse experiments in forms of choralization.

We have, first, Antonio Geraldo Figueiredo Ferreira's *As visitas que hoje estamos*.[10] Here, in this novel – a novel composed of segments so autonomous that they hardly read like a novel – resistance to formal categorization is announced from the outset, by the book's epigraphs: "all the voices all external not from the outside" (anonymous); "the novel is a kind of chorus of the deaf-mute where author and readers imagine themselves playing the role of the corypheus" (also anonymous); and "with the goods of some and the property of others, the common wealth is increased" (Machado de Assis). At work here is a kind of informal figuration of different voices, distinct in a regional sense; some evoke a world unfurling at a distance from the city, others make explicit their urban extraction. Generally speaking, these are monologues intentionally presented in pieces, chunks of life that seem to be in a kind of echo-dialogue with each other. But if this is the choral explicitly performed, the novel, on the other hand, offers other inventories, seemingly encyclopedic and fragmentary, archives, compilations of narrative forms, and exercises in the aphorismatic (involving the short poem, dramatic dialogue, the rubric, and the emblem).

Some of these inventories invoke, at times, Antonio Geraldo's invention of fictitious names for fictitious authors. *As visitas que hoje estamos* mentions, for instance, one book whose author is also named Antonio Geraldo, but with a very different last name (the real Antonio Geraldo's last name is Figueiredo Ferreira; the fictional one's is Levi). At some point, the novel even describes a page within it as if it were a kind of duplicate: a copy of the cover page of another (fictious) book. "No one wrote that," the page reads. One more fictitious writer, Eusébio Sousa, is described as the late author of a series of sophisms and a play (with incest as its dramatic engine and with constant reference to the world of Nelson Rodrigues' plays), which is perhaps the longest narrative sequence in the book and the only segment where we get closer to any kind of hypothetical closure. But the point is exactly its intentional non-hybridization. Different species of texts persist in their difference. There is no possible mix between them or unification.

Demonstration of the problematic juncture of the rural and the urban ("two realities, one and the same"); an attempt to re-read the Brazilian literary tradition; an act of compilation, a counterpoint to an effort at fraying – these are the lines running throughout this book. The same elements lead the author to revisit Machado de Assis, Guimarães Rosa, Graciliano Ramos, Nelson Rodrigues, Chico Alvim, and Dalton Trevisan, in acts of evident resumption and, importantly, of undeniable incompleteness, each one imbued with a certain nostalgia for forms that, as we well know, cannot be employed without a sense of working with intentional relics. The chorus in Antonio Geraldo's book points, simultaneously, to a certain community aspiration (belied by little acts of wickedness, here and there), toward the inclusiveness so anxiously hoped for by the social dashboard, and toward the limits of an epic smartly outlined and inevitably frayed and theatricalized.

Bernardo de Carvalho's *Reprodução* also opens with direct (and conflictive) references to a vocal kind of writing. "Listen to others to expand what you know," and "We only hear what we listen to, and we only listen to what interests us." The second epigraph invalidates, ironically, the notion of expansive, disinterested listening espoused by the first epigraph. And the invalidation continues in the monologue of the story's protagonist – a dull, reactionary character, a Chinese language student stopped by the authorities as he checks in for a flight. The book is in manifest dialogue with the work of André Sant'Anna (whose merits were perceived early by Carvalho), particularly with some of the narrators that Sant'Anna refers to as "famous anonymous imbeciles," which he once defined as "those who used 'to live in hiding, but who now, thanks to the internet, find themselves armed with their own opinions, ready to comment on websites, blogs, etc., always repeating preformed, usually imbecilic opinions."

It is that voice, the voice of the commonplace – the voice of a frequently conservative, authoritarian, prejudiced, racist, misogynist segment of public opinion – it is that voice that functions as a kind of scary choral figuration of the silent majority in the works of Sant'Anna. We hear its echoes in monologue-texts such as "Rush"[11] and "O importado vermelho de Noé."[12] We also hear it in longer narratives such as *Sexo* (1999),[13] a book driven by a kind of cliché-spurting textual machine – a machine strained, nonetheless, by difficult rhythmic constructions, marked by lists of indefatigable repetitions, formulaic expressions, and all manner of typification, brought together with the thinnest threads of plot.

We find, then, in the contrast between commonplaces and a demanding rhythm, a structure wherein choralization is defined not just by a plurality and an anonymity of voices (André's works may at first suggest this), but also, and especially, by means of riffing, of repetitions that sound almost the same but that are, in fact, distinguished by small internal variations: an ensemble-in-differentiation made up of almost identical segments. Elsewhere, we also find a certain rhythmic economy, just as demanding, as structural, but steered by voice and by the inflections of a voice – here, voice is elusive and individualized, as is the case in *Engano geográfico* by Marília Garcia.

Garcia's book is a narrative poem that moves between "he says," "she says," and "I heard a woman say," giving rise to a constant tension between first- and second-person storytelling, between declarations, hesitations, and interrogations. Speaking and listening are Garcia's horizons of writing in this book, and in it she presents readers with narrative exercises that have a foot outside the sphere of poetry but that are still best read attentively, as was the case with her previous book, *20 poemas para o seu Walkman* (2007). *Engano geográfico* is longer, and it expands the field of slippages (focal and geographical) and porosities (between cities, and between the multiple voices found in one single voice) already present in her earlier work. Slippages in this narrative poem are more than a way of moving around the story; they are constant readjustments of intonation and perception that dynamically configure the observations at the heart of the book.

O natimorto, by Lourenço Mutarelli, features a commodity-form (cigarette labels, with their health warnings and the grim images that often illustrate these warnings) presented as both collective enunciation and oracle. The series of stories narrated in the first person by the protagonist of the book (a musical agent who interprets, in his own way, the warnings on the cigarette labels, as if they were tarot cards) is in dialogue with this commodity-form, as is the sequence of dialogues between him and his protegée (a singer who's lost her voice, also a smoker). A succession of cigarettes, illustrations, and the discursive switching between health warnings, imagetic description, personal narrative, and conversations between two or three people: these are the elements, the back-and-forth between small verbal threads, that make up one of Mutarelli's best works to date. In it, Mutarelli manages to transform something which generally constitutes a compositional process completed in different languages (one graphic, one verbal, as is the case with comics) into a purely narrative fold. Mutarelli's book insinuates, mendaciously, that it, too, works like a comic book, alternating between verbal and graphic registers.

Delírio de damasco by Veronica Stigger also includes a kind of material transference: the boarding installed outside a SESC São Paulo (the one located on Avenida 24 de maio) for the 2010 exhibition of some of the texts included in her book. In the book as in the exhibition, both the verbal character of fragments of overheard conversation and the incomplete or invented sentences read similarly. But something about the diminutive scale of the printed text seems to evoke the feeling of a kind of secretive appropriation of street rumors, inappropriate and fanciful. This is signaled, again, by epigraphs bordering on the contradictory: one by De Quincey (on the ominous ring of some overheard phrases) and another by Oswald de Andrade (on how one writes about what's heard and never about what happens). The book is composed entirely with voices and is thus in manifest dialogue with Andrade's appropriations and with the choral poetry of Chico Alvim. It signals the relevance of the ready-made approach to composition in Stigger's writing – as in "Destinos" (a poem extracted from the list of São Paulo bus routes), "Luana" (from the book *Gran Cabaret Demenzial*, 2007), the entire section titled "Histórias da arte" from the book *Os anões* (2010), and in her frequent use of advertisements, housekeeping advice, and the period illustrations that erupt, from time to time, in the novel *Opisanie Swiata* (2013). They stay there, loose, disjointed, floating around, untethered, almost thing-like, just like the book characters Bopp, Mr. Andrade, and Opalka, whose obligatory tracing creates a kind of relief and roughness in a narrative that wishes to present itself in a self-ironic, deceptively light, plain, and flat way. The novel literally laughs at those who believe in a proper place for a writer, in a proper – elevated in mode, homogeneously epic, conventionally accepted – way of treating a novel.

Now, let´s approach one more time Nuno Ramos, both his writings and artworks. In his artworks, he also uses appropriations, but with materials that don't usually mix, that collide. The appropriations don't tend toward embossment – they melt, sink, crash, and crumble. If these appropriations can function as collections of fragile objects (such as in *Globo da morte de tudo*, 2012) or of remnants of houses (*Ai, pareciam eternas!* [*3 Lamas*], 2012), what dominates in these works are materials of visibly conflicting textures. His writings include fragments of tragic choruses (*Mar Morto*, 2008), texts of various origins (*Carolina*, 2006), and samples of popular music (*Vai vai e Choro negro*, 2004). These materials appear with increasing frequency in his installations, and frequently have verbal consistency of some kind. Everything seems to speak in his work.[14]

These choral figurations, in his case, point to a kind of critical restraint to the very objectification of the works, and to a process of formalization, dramatized and re-dramatized with each new work. And they signal, simultaneously, the recurrent choralities found in recent Brazilian cultural life that point to perceivable efforts of figuration, of listening to a collective rumor still lacking a distinct social shape. It's an effort presented, at times, in a spectral kind of way, as "absent community" (to use the words of Martin Mégevand). At other times, it emerges as an active lack that, in the literary field, is intensified by processes of redefinition driven by different forms of choral practice, of the kind experienced during the unfoldings of the 2013 *Jornadas de Junho* (which served as background for the first draft of this reflection).

3

Artistic Actions / Political Actions (Before and After Rousseff's Impeachment)

It is hardly surprising that one of the most meaningful literary responses to the political dynamic of Brazil's dark hour during the Dilma Rousseff impeachment process – and to what came after[1] – re-engaged, quietly but strategically, a textual model that was (and evidently continues to be) paradigmatic in the constitution of Brazilian literature: songs of exile. I am calling attention here to a poem by Angélica Freitas. A poem that straightforwardly points to a very specific place and time is "porto alegre, 2016," written, as the poem suggests, in Berkeley, California, on May 14, 2016. It was originally published as a stand-alone poem, with no remarks beyond the poem, in a blog linked to the poetry magazine *Modo de Usar*.[2]

Strictly speaking, the poem had no title, but the page where it was published included a photograph by Caco Argemi and the following caption: "Cavalry charge, with swords drawn, by the 4th Mounted Patrol Unit."[3] The photograph shows a law enforcement action that took place on Friday, May 13, 2016,[4] in Cidade Baixa, in the Brazilian city of Porto Alegre, during a protest organized to denounce the impeachment of Dilma Rouseff.

This chapter was first published as an essay, following an invitation extended by Schneider Carpeggiani, for the December 2016 and January 2017 issues of *Suplemento Pernambuco*, where it first appeared.

Although the scene is only described in a more explicit manner in the last stanza of the poem, the photograph still functions as a constant visual reference throughout the poem as published in *Modo de Usar*. Its simple presence on the page – and in news circulating all over Brazil around that time – seems to haunt the other sections of the poem. The local police action silently overshadows all the repressive actions discussed throughout the poem, which, conversely, point to different parts of the globe.

The first three stanzas of the poem share a similar structure. They start with the same repeated expression offering alarm at the sight of a clash – "quando você viu" ("when have you ever seen") – followed by a description of various kinds of clashes. Invariably, the poem highlights the distance between the subject witnessing these clashes on a screen and the scenes they witness – a distance underlined using a kind of self-addressed second person ("have you ever") instead of an immediate first-person point of view.

Migrants ("those people lined up in the rain / at night, on a road / at the border, in a country that no longer needs them") are mentioned in the first stanza. Pronouns are vague, deliberately so, to suggest that the people mentioned in the section could be anyone, that the road they walk and the country they're in could be anywhere. In the second stanza, we see "bombs / falling on distant cities," and once again the poem calls attention to houses and streets – "so dirty and so peculiar," reminiscent of so many places. And yet the poem suggests both distance and difference. The words indicate a "there" observed by a distant "here." Like in the nineteenth-century – and modern – Brazilian songs of exile,[5] the opposition between here and there, homeland and foreign places, is crucial to the imagery constructed by the poem. The next stanza places us again in some foreign country, where we witness police attacking protesters with tear gas.

By the third segment of the poem, the reference to one of the poles of geographic alterity that characterizes songs of exile becomes explicit: the foreign territory. And so, a distant "over there" is constructed, through repetition and eventually in opposition to a closer "out there" that begins to take shape over the course of the next three stanzas. A sense of estrangement builds up, a negation, underscored with each verse – "didn't think twice / didn't change the channel"; "didn't notice what was coming"; "didn't interpret the news as a sign"; "didn't feel the need to stock up on supplies." The distant, the remote, the foreign start to seem a short distance away. And then, in the last segment of the poem, violence comes closer, and estrangement is replaced by astonishment: "and the noise of the bomb is right outside / and the police goes full force on your affects; armed with swords, mounted on horses."

It seems then that, by the end of the poem, Caco Argemi's photograph has infiltrated the poem. The spatial demarcation, the otherness, the figuration from a distance of different places and conflicts, and the opposition between a "here" and a "there" – characteristic of songs of exile – now underline a series of layered scenes of violence that, at this moment, emphasize an overlapping of violent patterns. They also reveal more convergences than the bipolar territorializations of nationality demanded by the nineteenth-century geographical imagination used to suggest.

The global scale of the violent scenes of exclusion unfolding in Freitas' poem announce, in a kind of exemplary polyptych, a sense of astonishment as well as a growing consciousness about the shared local dimension of a worldview that, until then, had taken shape only indirectly, through TV screens, and from a bird's-eye view. Through distant cities, then, through the eyes of strangers standing in line waiting for border inspections, through the perspective of protesters gathered in a plaza in some foreign city, we move toward an "out there," a "right out there" that suddenly makes itself present. Our jaws drop, and just like that, prosaically, we see and sense the force immersing us in historical experience.

Artwork and critical research take place in necessary dialogue with the present moment. But when democratic institutionality – like the one that had been in a process of reconstruction in Brazil in the three decades prior to Rousseff's impeachment – finds itself destabilized, this dialogue and the engagement it entails are deliberately intensified. Moments in which democratic institutions were destabilized have also intensified the relationship between politics and culture in recent Brazilian criticism and art production. This became particularly evident when we started to see clearly the ultraconservative unfoldings of the *Jornadas* of 2013; the depth of the ideological divide that split (and continues to split) the nation; and the potential for virulence embedded in that division, a virulence manifest both around and beyond any election campaign, exacerbated and spreading over every aspect of life, of coexistence. What had been, until then, a kind of collective premonition took shape and expanded into an everyday experience, especially in the months leading up to the impeachment, and in the months that followed.

In Brazil, in the nineteenth century as well as in many modernist examples of the genre (and in more recent iterations written during the years of military dictatorship), songs of exile function as artifacts to examine the notion of nationality. The fact that artists started revisiting these songs, these textual models, not only points to a movement toward an emerging consciousness about the present circumstance; it also indicates a sense of discomfort in relation to both the nation and the imposition of a new/old order as signaled in Freitas' poem.

Revisiting these songs also points to actual exiles and disorientations. We see this, for example, in the deliberately diffuse geography of works such as Luiza Baldan's *Perabé* (2015), a video installation composed of photographs and an audio narration (in four voices) that retrace a crossing through São Paulo to see the sea without really leaving its non-coastal landscape. It starts in the Cantareira Mountains, and, led by diverse characters, stories, and travel accidents, the artist finally reaches a neighborhood called Marapé (formerly Perabé), which in Tupi language means "way of the sea." From a very different perspective, but also working with methodic deterritorializations, we can evoke the distinctive temporal layering (of caravels, colonial garb, and contemporary figures) emblematic of the work of the painter Arjan Martins. Or we can turn inward and observe these disorientations in the unfolding of the self. "I is a rhinoceros a hippopotamus – / suddenly I was everywhere / everywhere / and in a box ..."[6] – that is how the subject describes and dissolves himself in Franklin Dassie's poem "Grandes mamíferos."[7] "Me whom / no one" ("Mim quem / nin guém"), we read in a poem by Chacal. These are inner exiles that, for good reason, call forth processes of formalization structured by methodical fissures (spatial, temporal, and figural).

If we assess Brazilian cultural production in the 2010s for its potential for invention and for the vigor of its dialogue with the historical moment, works characterized, at one and the same time, by convergent and antagonistic configurations (by the elaboration of tense, confrontational expressive fields) stand out as particularly significant. Sometimes these works are (openly or potentially) belligerent, violent, as in the Chernobyl series and the minefields series by Alice Miceli,[8] or in the images of explosions by the Minas Gerais artist Lais Myrrha.[9] Sometimes they dwell on frank devastation, like all the segments of Carlito Azevedo's poem "Book of the Dog."

These are the kind of conflictive structured configurations I want to follow here. Especially along the lines of four distinct series: imprecise presents; scenes involving fictive voices and voices *a vero*; walls (as matter and as a limit); and dogs (dead dogs, ferocious dogs, dogs that stray), the canine figures sometimes functioning as authorial doubles and sometimes as antagonists – inclement guardians that seem to announce or to make effective a progressive besiegement of either citizenship or the simple ability to move freely, to come and go as one pleases.

Precise Imprecise Presents[10]

From its beginning, in the impeachment process against Dilma Rousseff, one notion – historical repetition – has proven crucial in every effort to describe the contemporary experience of institutional destabilization. Repetition here does not mean exact repetition, and yet, understandably, it comes across as shocking when the terms in question are, on the one hand, the military dictatorship that seized power in 1964 and, on the other hand, the authoritarian judicial and political apparatus of Brazil in the in 2010s. Repetition also links the palace coup that instituted the Brazilian "República Velha" (1889–1930), the subsequent various political disruptions, and the articulations that led to an impeachment in 2016 (despite the absence of any imputable crime). Repetition in the way I mean is also relevant when we consider the link between recent events in Brazilian politics and the series of destabilizing processes unleashed against left-leaning or center-left governments in Latin America: Venezuela in 2002–3; Haiti in 2004; Bolivia in 2008; Ecuador in 2010 (three other such processes, in Honduras, Paraguay, and Brazil, resulted in the removal of executives).

Historical repetition as a means of understanding the present also includes examining the use of political rhetoric recontextualized by those usurping the state apparatus and by the Brazilian mainstream press before and after Rousseff's impeachment. This examination intensifies the perception of curious near re-editions of newspaper front pages and articles from the 1960s in current contexts like the ones discussed below. They include modernized versions of anti-corruption propaganda used by conservative politicians of the past, such as Jânio Quadros' "little broom" (insinuating unproven dishonesty in the Kubitschek administration) as well as the image of the "sea of mud" extracted from speeches by a right-wing politician (Carlos Lacerda). Recent historical repetitions, however, erase the original anti-Getúlio Vargas or anti-João Goulart context from which they originated, despite the fact that they redeploy past images and speeches almost verbatim against new labor or leftist politicians.

Tracking these repetitions – with Marx's *The Eighteenth Brumaire of Louis Bonaparte* as their vanishing point – allows us to point, simultaneously, to both the farcical nature of these duplications (which barely have any sense of conviction about themselves, as Paul Laurent Assoun points out) and the impossibility of simply re-editing anything in the face of changing historical and material conditions. While this strategy of observing the dissimilarities of the apparently similar seeks to expose the mismatch between refigurations like the ones described above, it also points to the need for a growing awareness of the singularities of the present. This need is particularly urgent when these singularities are haunted by various, conservative attempts at restoration, and numerous attempted returns to authoritarian practices, including the prospect of revoking both individual and labor rights as well as the post-1988 achievements of civil society through the Brazilian Constitution (such as broader access to education and healthcare and its democratic advances).

A recent comic strip from an André Dahmer series titled "Os malvados" ("The Evil Ones") synthesized these temporal tensions in three frames picturing scenes of going back in history, but with language that points to a present, immediate political agenda. The first one exposes a movement of temporal regression: "The past has returned to Brazil." The second seeks to discern exactly what has been allowed to return: "Did you bring anything from abroad?" And the last one makes explicit, through the shortest of replies, the cruel, violent, character of this anachronizing dimension: "A whip." Like the ones used during the slavery period. The heart of the satiric potential of the strip – anchored graphically in the angelic portrait of the evil characters, and verbally in their capacity for synthesis – intensified by Dahmer's commitment to present matters – lies in its title: "Labor Reform" ("Reforma trabalhista"). Indeed, the comic strip's superimposition of a discussion on labor rights, on the one hand, and the memory of slavery, on the other hand, is what gives rise to its political dimension.

Temporal, imagistic, or contextual overlaps have proven fundamental in artistic processes aimed, equally, at intensifying their potential for dissent. This is observed, as already noted, in the painting by Arjan Martins, with his upside-down caravels evoking the period of slavery. We also see it in José Luiz Passos' historical novel, *O Marechal de costas* (2016), informed as it is by both historical folds and insertions from the present. The overlays in Passos' novel can be seen in the way a mirroring in its plot (between the First Brazilian Republic and present-day Brazil) is conjugated with the focal contrast between two characters (the semi-documentary Marechal Floriano Peixoto and a fictional present-day cook). The narrative operation at work in Passos' novel seems to be invested in structured, temporal intersections similar to the more unpredictable ones that give shape to fictions such as *Viagem ao Mexico* (1995) and *Em Liberdade* (1994) by Silviano Santiago.

Contrary to the approach Passos takes in his dialogue with the historical novel, what guides the appropriation of Tom Jobim and Newton Mendonça's song "Samba de uma nota só" in Nuno Ramos' installation *O direito à preguiça* (2016) is a decisive non-historicism. The same can be said of Eryk Rocha's documentary film called *Cinema novo*, evoked previously in "Regarding the Chorus," where he reexamines the moment in the history of Brazilian cinema referenced in the title of his film. The two works, however, involve both the construction of dialogues across different moments in time and the interference between different periods of Brazilian cultural and political life, emphasizing – in these intersections – a very strong interpellation of the present.

In Nuno's work, installed during the first half of 2016 at the Centro Cultural Banco do Brasil (CCBB) in Belo Horizonte, a scaffolding around 15 meters tall and connected to 106 organ tubes played a mournful, virtually unrecognizable version of

Jobim and Mendonça's bossa nova song, reimagined by Leandro Cesar and Nuno Ramos, and delivered very slowly, on a loop, incessantly repeated by a wall of sound. The choice of the song is anything but random. It is one of the most paradigmatic songs in the bossa nova repertoire, and among the most beautiful works of twentieth-century Brazilian popular music. But it necessarily evokes almost immediately the "developmentalism" of the Juscelino Kubitschek government, the optimism linked to the modernization of that period, the middle class from which the musical movement evolved, and the songs full of sunny images and visions of a relatively carefree daily life in Rio de Janeiro. By way of contrast, the installation also included other sound walls featuring an audio recording from the auction of Munch's *The Scream*, as well as a recording featuring Carlos Drummond de Andrade reading his own poem "José," where he stresses: "the party is over," "the lights are off," "people went home," "laughter never took hold," "utopia didn't happen," "and everything broke loose," "and everything now full of mold" ("a festa acabou," "a luz apagou," "o povo sumiu," "o riso não veio," "não veio a utopia," "e tudo fugiu," "e tudo mofou").

The market register of ever increasing prices for Munch's painting; the disenchantment, the repeated refiguration in "José" of the question "what can you do about it" ("o que fazer") mediated by the voice of Drummond; and, most of all, the hyper-deceleration of Jobim's song produced by the immense wall of sound erected in the patio of Belo Horizonte's CCBB: all this suggested, as you passed through it, a disjointed time where the utopia represented by the picture-perfect, bossa nova middle class of 1950s Brazil allows itself to be occupied by a different scaffolding, by another (mournful) music score, making room for negativity and for the contradictory dimension of a kind of dystopian foreboding.

In *Cinema novo*, Eryk Rocha's work is driven by a deliberate non-superimposition of contemporary materials onto scenes from classic Brazilian films from the *cinema novo* movement and archival footage concerning the same period. Everything we see on screen is appropriated matter, and contemporary insertion happens by means of a rhythm: an/other rhythm which refigures both the object and its time, the way it happens in Ramos' *O direito à preguiça*. However, if in Rocha's work, as in Ramos' wall-organ, there is a suggestion of a *perpetuum mobile*, the speed in Rocha's work is necessarily different: not the (purposely) extremely slow mourning of Ramos' sound sculpture but a *prestissimo* kind of movement. This is the result of the remarkable montage work completed by the director in collaboration with Renato Vallone. They spliced together over 100 films and reconstituted them into a set of vertiginous series – people running, kisses, struggles, open spaces, pain. The flux is nonstop, but we experience it as the present tense of film, which, in its own peculiar time, leads directly to a reflection on film and Brazil in the 1960s, seemingly and simultaneously wondering about the present moment and the different possible ways of thinking through the nation by means of cinema. Here are a present-in-flux and a film with a choreographic dimension that, in exacting synchronicity but without offering any kind of reading key, seems to demand from that other present – contemporary Brazil – the reconstruction (necessarily in movement) of its artistic and political motivations, during a period that is as somber as it is potent.

Walls, Palimpsests, Pentimenti

This strategic exercise in contrastive superimposition and contextual contamination is not limited to the temporal dimension. It has also been fundamental in occupations, roadblocks, and flash mobs, as well as in sudden interventions (sometimes in the form of text or image projections) in public spaces and high-transit areas, interventions mounted as responses that are immediately more effective against projects and initiatives linked both to gentrification and to the restriction of rights that had been increasingly enforced in Brazil in the absence of any kind of popular referendum.

Territories are thus created within other territories, and it is up to the new ones to temporarily or more permanently define the old ones. Examples of this include the "Ocupe Estelita" movement, which converted the José Estelita wharf in downtown Recife into a protest site – a site for urban rights and against real estate speculation. The force of this site seems to be beautifully and fictively mirrored in the film *Aquarius* (2016) by Kléber Mendonça Filho. It also resonates with "Ocupa Minc-RJ," which transformed the Rio de Janeiro headquarters of the Ministry of Culture at the Palácio Gustavo Capanema (which was then being renovated) into a center for the production and discussion of cultural practices and new forms of thinking about politics. Other examples include the student occupations that started in São Paulo in 2015 opposing school closures and forcible student transfers (measures proposed by the São Paulo state administration of Geraldo Alckmin). More of these protests emerged in 2016, in hundreds of institutions (including private institutions), as gestures of resistance against the high school education reforms that President Temer tried to impose (through a so-called Medida Provisória), and in opposition to PEC-55, which mandated an extremely worrisome and perverse reduction of the already inadequate public health and education systems in Brazil. Add to this the short-term occupations of legislative assemblies and diverse acts of urban intervention: people ripping apart electoral ballots, or tearing out pages of the 1988 Constitution; people satirically restaging scenes from the parliamentary impeachment process in places where this kind of critique would be perceived as hostile, for example in a march organized by the "Teatro pela Democracia" group, which took place on a sunny Sunday on Avenida Atlântica in Copacabana, Rio de Janeiro. Yet another example is the flash mob (staged in several sites across Rio de Janeiro) against impeachment organized by Patrick Sampaio as part of the "Reage Artista" movement, in which a woman passing out was immediately mimicked by dozens of other people passing out after her.

Intentional re-activations of the form of the protest encampment – characteristic of the occupations of land, mills, and abandoned buildings carried out by both the landless workers' movements and the homeless workers' movements – are clearly evident in these more recent occupations. This method has been increasingly adopted in Brazil, especially since the 1990s. Alongside this dialogue with Brazilian political history, there is also an incorporation of constitutive aspects of Occupy movements taking place elsewhere in the world (for instance, the Occupy Wall Street movement, and the 15-M/Indignados movement in Spain) in response to a diverse range of circumstances (economic, environmental, social) and linked to international anti-globalization movements.

Recent occupations also make use of cumulative procedures like those employed by artistic installations, which frequently leads to complex intersections between references to contemporary art, on the one hand, and the use of the encampment form, on the other. Singular actions and interventions with a precise, immediate focus also evidently demonstrate very strong connections between art actions and political acts, theater, performance, graffiti, street art, and the critical exercise of both citizenship and free movement through diverse areas of a city.

If occupations maintain the tension between, on the one hand, the spaces they appropriate and, on the other hand, the re-functionalization they bring about, and if that is the contrast that amplifies their potential for problematization, urban interventions can also be said to be necessarily in dialogue with spatial ordering and everyday social divisions – exposing, however, these divisions to the displacements that result from unforeseen events. This can leave behind traces in the urban memory, as happened after the occupation of the "Túnel Novo" passage in Rio de Janeiro (the tunnel that connects the Botafogo and Copacabana neighborhoods) by people taking part in an alternative opening ceremony for the 2016 Olympics; or after the night-time soccer game organized in 2013 in Avenida Delfim Moreira by teams formed both by activists obstructing the entrance of a building in protest against Sérgio Cabral Filho (ex-governor of the state of Rio de Janeiro) and by protesters who came down from impoverished hillside neighborhoods to denounce the disappearance of Amarildo de Souza, a bricklayer seized by the Pacifying Police Unit (Unidade de Polícia Pacificadora, UPP) on his way home from the supermarket. These events stay behind, they remain present, like active layers in the political imaginary and in discussions about urban rights, like geographic–temporal palimpsests where new spheres of action are inscribed.

Exercises in street art and pictorial writing by artists such as Joana Cesar, Gustavo Speridião, and Alexandre Vogler are in visible dialogue with these kinds of interventions. They are also in dialogue with the "city of walls" (to use a term coined by Teresa Pires Caldeira) pattern of seclusion that now defines the largest metropolitan areas in Brazil, with their increasing privatization of public space and their employment of techniques of security and residential, commercial, and institutional fortification – the same metropolitan areas that now have walls and fences as truly exemplary images of an exacerbation both of fear and of the politics of control and social segregation. Walls also function as crucial materials in the artistic (and diverse) processes of Joana Cesar and Gustavo Speridião. They appear not just as safeguarded territories (open, nonetheless, to intervention), but also as cumulative supports, where layers and layers of previous inscriptions are stored. A stark contrast is visible, for instance, between the image of the walled city and the urban inscriptions of Alexandre Vogler, which occupy vertical spaces (warning, for instance, against the removal of poor people from Rio de Janeiro's affluent Zona Sul) and horizontal spaces alike: on beaches (for example, as part of an intervention where he wrote the words "A / trair / investimento" ["Attract / Betray / Investment"] directly in the sand) and on sidewalks ("Fui mijar sumi no mar" ["I went to pee I got lost at sea"] carved into concrete). Speridião and Joana, on their part, cultivate a truly imposing relationship with the texture, the choral aspect, and the accumulation of vestiges found on public walls.

Speridião's work includes insertions in urban space, such as his *Nuvens*, a series of cube-clouds dating back to 2005 and scattered around Rio's port area. Since 2019, mostly during the Bolsonaro administration, Gustavo Speridião and Leandro Barboza created "FAIXA PROTESTA," large-scale paintings and poetry of rebellion exhibited and used during protests and marches. Most common, however, are Speridião's appropriations of "world images" from graphic media and from anonymous individual and collective sources found on the street. Sometimes he appropriates pages torn from books that he renames, adding commentaries, margins, and ironic captions, as seen, for instance, in the series titled "O Fantástico e Inabitável Mundo da História da Arte" (2005–13). Sometimes they constitute larger works, collages made with posters and pamphlets. It is, however, his methodic use of painting as pentimento that draws particular attention to his work. Painting as support for the calculated tension between composition and manifestation, as a layer-procedure where letters, diverse forms, political slogans, irregular stanzas, and meeting minutes of political gatherings are superimposed and placed into conflict. Sometimes these elements are frankly autoreferential (e.g. *Uma pausa**, *A rigorosa paisagem*, *Estrofe irregular*, and *Linear captura Pictórico*); other times, they evoke calls to action and point to the (direct) political dimension found within/outside the work (as in *Maldita burguesia*; *Não*; *Fora*; *O mundo periculoso* *do trabalho*; *Não temer o mundo. Mudá-lo*; *Amanhã manifestação*). The diction of the call to action is present even when the visual reference to the street, the poster, or the wall finds itself tensed by an intimate kind of expression (*Queria estar tranquilo*, *A lágrima é só suor do cérebro*) or when, almost silently, it underlines, negatively but still with the force of a slogan, his artistic method (*Pare com as frases*).

In Joana Cesar's work, if the street plays a propelling role – as the "ideal support for an anonymous work," as she likes to say – it is textures, layers, and the "sensation of accumulation" of walls that contributes decisively to the constitution of a singular poetic. These elements operate as the field of tension for her street paintings (structured as they are by simplified human forms and by the enlarged scale of letters from a codified alphabet), in contrast with other urban manifestations such as graffiti, posters, and the whitewashing used by municipal authorities to cover up inscriptions on public walls.

The immense texts by Joana Cesar, painted in an alphabet invented by the artist and scattered throughout Rio de Janeiro, look like adverts; they look like announcements even though they're undecipherable for the passer-by. Sometimes, when they're installed in larger spaces, they acquire new narrative dimensions. The ones installed on the columns of the elevated Avenida Perimetral were distributed in symmetrical visual diptychs that occupied the thoroughfare while also standing as a kind of lament in the face of the demolition of the elevated avenue and other transformations that took place in Rio's port area in anticipation of the 2016 Olympics. The artist described these inscriptions as the mourning monologue spoken by a composite figure – part lizard, part elevated highway – as it lays dying.

More than a decade of continuous street painting experience ended up having an impact on Joana's studio work. It grew in scale (in line with her mural works) and became characterized by a compositional process completed in layers. In general, she works with larger canvases where fragments of photos, documents, advertisements, segments of billboards, letters, plaster pieces, and all kinds of printed matter are cut and arranged into what the artist calls different "thematic areas / islands."

"Memory is in the layers; they tell the story of the surface presented," the painter once explained in an interview to *Revista*

Usina[11] in 2014. It's an observation that's fundamental to her poetics, different from Speridião's but with a shared understanding of painting as a practice of writing and layering. As Marcos Siscar states in a poem from *Manual de flutuação para amadores* (2015), "... what was used does not need / to be recycled rebound as new / what comes from use lacks having been / occupied rewritten as the first book / of a curious genre exposed to fracture / in times of crisis of nothing dies down / or just that a desire of a world."[12] What's made present here, in this stanza and in the large canvases Joana Cesar paints, is a process of construction through occupation, cutting, and also superimposition, by means of which what is in fact exposed are not simply forms, colors, or writings (writings that remain present), but the very sensation of accumulation and its force.

Figural Folds, Intra-differentiations

Public and private walls, urban fences and barriers also impose themselves on recent Brazilian literary culture. Sometimes as topical figurations of limits and exclusions, sometimes as support structures exposed to regular interventions of varying intensity, or to successive layers of vestiges, materials, textures, and urban echoes. They can even emerge as hypotheses, and where you least expect them, in equally unexpected forms, the way they do in Marília Garcia's "Paris não tem centro" (2016).

In Garcia's long poem, they appear in the middle of the story of a return trip to São Paulo, in the register of the discomfort caused by "speaking within an institution," given how, in the narrative present of the poem, "it is very dangerous to talk about institutions / later they can use that against you." It is exactly in that moment of explicit fear that, suddenly, you can visualize walls emerging in the poem. Not literal walls, but walls in the form of a proposal, much like Sol Lewitt's wall drawings: instructions by the artist on how to make drawings on walls, interventions whose result necessarily depends, however, on who follows these instructions and how these instructions are followed. In Garcia's case the wall is, then, a kind of hypothetical response – a suspended one – to acts of moving through institutional territories that feel increasingly fearsome.

These walls can also impose themselves as barriers that suddenly and unavoidably stand in one's way. An example of this is Franklin Dassie's poetic series "Casaco de Moletom com Capuz"[13] ("Hoodie"), where an archive (almost like a moving wall) is counterposed to the barely noticeable movements of a subject. In the series, Dassie seems to be invariably passing through "a giant archive" – "that thing resembling life" or a "natural history museum" – until there is "no more home / just a large room / a giant archive / that I always walk through." A cumulative succession of barriers: in Dassie's poetry, this is one among several hindrances by means of which his poems are constantly disassembled and put back together. They can turn into episodic game series; sometimes there are boxes, sometimes oranges, rhinos, hippopotamuses, sometimes names and addresses – confused, multiplied. They can also unfold into a sequence of falls involving lost forms, documents, papers, certificates. This can take place on the street, in the gutter, on the grass, in the car glove compartment, or inside the head of the person carrying all these things.

Consciously working through walls, archives, layers, and the different ways of using all these objects is par for the course during somber times. Interventions and occupations in restrictive spaces; appropriations of 1960s Brazilian films in Eryk Rocha's *Cinema novo* documentary film; the extremely slow speeds at which "Samba de uma nota só" is played in Nuno Ramos' *O direito à preguiça*; the exercise in refiguration (with the negative "over there") Angélica Freitas performs in her dialogue with songs of exile: all of these are examples of this form of working-through. In the spheres of theater and narrative, this unfolds into interventions on the very manner of constructing a voice – in figurations and narratorial dictions subjected to an intense process of intra-differentiation.

Along these lines, two theatrical productions from Ceará, both linked to the trans universe (*Histórias compartilhadas*, 2015, and *BR Trans*, 2015) strike me as particularly exemplary. While each adopts a rather different set of procedures, both maintain a calculated tension between the characters interviewed or recorded for each of these projects and the performer behind the (multifocal) monologue that runs through each play.

BR Trans, on its part, works with a vast sequence of stories, and each new story is made singular in a process that consists in the actor Silvero Pereira inscribing a feminine name (Bruna, Mika, Babi, Marcelly, Tyna, Milena, Dani) on his body for every new story that comes into play. This already makes evident a sense of differentiation between character and narrator; it already highlights a distinction between character and narrator. But it also includes vocal duplications or dubbing of other people's voices (such as that of the singer Maria Bethânia).

In *Histórias Compartilhadas*, a play originally developed as a university capstone project, Ari Areia and Eduardo Bruno opt for an intentionally more distanced form of presentation, one that also does not rely on any attempt to mimetically appropriate the universe evoked by the project. In this work, amid a series of stories linked to male transexual life (the stories of João W. Nery, Otávio Queiroz, Tiago Uchoa, Riley Moscatel, and Buck Angel), what is most emphasized and developed is a contrast between documentary theater and the composition (by Ari Areia) of a performance, in parallel to the stories captured on video. The performance includes moments when the body is exposed to pain, to discomfort, but this is done in a methodical way, almost silently. Blood is drawn on stage and then dripped over an image of Jesus Christ. This, of course, resulted in judicial investigations and physical threats to the author, rerouting the transphobic dimension of the reactions to the work to another sphere: the sphere of a supposedly religious quarrel.

Within the realm of these intra-differentiated appropriations of the voices and stories of others, the method employed by Bia Lessa and Dany Roland in a film that took them almost two decades to complete – *Então morri* (2016) – is radically different. The film was never screened commercially, only in festivals in Rio de Janeiro and São Paulo. It is anchored on the construction of a life story, the story of a woman who is also a legion. The film is made using fragments of the lives of a series of women at different stages in life – young women, older women, girls, dead women. The basis of the work is a succession of testimonies gathered in transit through different Brazilian cities.

There is no commentary or any other intervention to try and stitch together these fragments; only the voices of the different women appear on screen, assembling, collectively, the life of a woman. Differences, however, are not dissipated; on the contrary, brute heterogeneity is crucial. Also key to the film is the way it makes evident the presence of two cameras and the fact that they are operated by outsiders, relative to the places they observe. The cameras are always in movement, in explicit contrast to the slow rhythm of the lives of the women portrayed and of the small cities they inhabit.

In the plays discussed above, there is a clear (albeit emphatic) demarcation of the differentiations that stand between distinct testimonies, and between those testimonies and the locus of performance of those who explicitly perform. In *Então morri*, the fiction of a life feeds, documentarily, from heterogeneities kept as such. The film doesn't care much about emphasizing demarcations, it keeps its rhythm moving from woman to woman, from life to life, constructing a kind of internally dissimilar "Everywoman."

By contrast, in texts like *O Brasil é bom* (2014) by André Sant'Anna, for example, deliberate detachment and repulsion make way for either the enraged or the allegedly illuminated (in a juridical or a religious way) discourse of the mostly conservative segment of the Brazilian middle class. In this apparent mimetic concession of the voice (and of discursive articulation) to a new working class devoid of class consciousness, and to an increasingly virulent middle class (individualist and incapable of thinking without mediatic fireworks and repetitions of religious and neoliberal clichés), Sant'Anna intensifies the sense of distance. A pseudo-naïve and enraged voice is theatricalized in a manner so close to its habitual way of speaking that it is hard to see, on first reading, the satiric intelligence of a writer who is perhaps among the most important in contemporary Brazilian literature. Along with that approximation, we also find a rhythmic reconstruction that exposes these ways of speaking to the point of exhaustion, where they achieve a level of self-repetition that is also erosion, inclement disassembly.

Intra-differentiations that undermine seemingly homogeneous or controllably heterogeneous dictions can also directly target the functioning of the literary field, its discursive disputes, and the possibilities of authorial self-representation. Recall, for instance, a book such as *As visitas que hoje estamos* by Antonio Geraldo Figuereiro Ferreira, constructed with parallel discursive layers. Recall, also, *Inquérito policial: Família Tobias* (2016) by Ricardo Lisias.

The first novel is an inquiry into both the loss of force in literary writing ("How did Brazil get to a number of novels so large they stopped troubling anyone?" – as we read in Antonio Geraldo's book) and calculated authorial exposure. The second book looks into the control mechanisms of a judicialized society where individual rights are passively ceded, including the very right to show dissent without the possibility of facing criminal charges. What Lisias did was to put together, in digitally published serials, a judicial fiction that would lead him to an actual intimation and to the composition of a non-narrative that literally assumes the form and the rhetoric of a criminal inquiry, thus exposing, simultaneously, the reasoning and the cognitive and discursive limits of this format and of a logic that, when coupled with a simplified religious imaginary, seems to feed both neoconservatism and the call to "order and segregation" that rings expansively around Brazil.

In a similar style to Lisias' book-inquiry, another writer, João Paulo Cuenca, constructed what is perhaps his best novel, titled *Descobri que estava morto* (2016), a sprawling dialogue with police discourse. In his case, the ironic exercise in autofiction is cruel, extremely cruel. Between the tedium of predictable aspects of literary life and an almost involuntary involvement (in the book) in urban protests, the narrative transforms into a vigorous, heat-of-the-moment inquiry into artistic experience in times of both democratic recession and expanding normalization of the state of exception. In this sense, the final segments of the novel, the violent confrontations both with law enforcement and with the narrator's own historical hour, constitute a kind of perverse twist on the protocols of autofiction, its usual discussion of fact and fiction. They lead the narrator to expose himself not just as a split figure, but as a dead end.

The Dog

It is hardly a coincidence that, at a certain point during the anatomy of the narrator performed by Cuenca, this same narrator falls into a pit filled with blood and shards of glass, the taste of teargas (courtesy of the police) filling his mouth. Dogs begin to lick his face. The beatings the narrator suffers in the novel are the result of his more or less random exposure to urban conflict; the same can't be said about the presence of dogs. This presence seems even less of a coincidence in recent cultural production. There are, for instance, some almost imperceptible barking sounds in *Então morri*, the Bia Lessy and Dany Roland film. There is also the caged *Pitbull*, depicted in a cruelly realist way, in a painting by Jorge Duarte from 2013. More examples include the dogs that appear in some images of *Perabé* (2014–5) by Luiza Baldán, mentioned earlier, or the ones that emerge in paintings by Arjan Martins, or the fundamental *Monólogo para um cachorro morto* (2008) by Nuno Ramos.

The dogs that approach the wounded body of the narrator in *Descobri que estava morto* seem friendly, empathetic, but this is almost never the case. Witness, for instance, the following scene in "Sem Vagas," a short story by Ricardo Domeneck: "Now the dog starts barking in the courtyard of the house next door. BEWARE DOG. You're not welcome here." "And who is?" asks the narrator. Augusto de Campos plays around with a similar kind of warning in a pre-impeachment intervention where, in a deliberate superimposition of time frames, he appropriates the mosaic found in Pompey's House of the Tragic Poet: "Cave canem" ("Beware of Dog"). But the text found in Pompey becomes CAVE MIDiA$ or "Beware of the M€DIA." The warning here includes dogs but also Midas–Media, as well as those who control capital. With his extraordinary gift for synthesis, Campos combines a series of other dogs with the Pompey one, imposing on it the confluence of plutocracy, uncritical mass media, and police repression that tends to sustain authoritarian regimes.

The dog that walks around in the canine-operatic prologue included in Carlito Azevedo's *Livro das postagens* (2016) is a bitchy figure, bloodied and at the limit. It's a dog inhabited by others: the dogs in Godard's *Goodbye to Language* (2014), Marina Tsvetaeva's dog, the dogs in drawings by Maiakovski, and the nocturnal song of Augusto de Campos' white whale ("Cançãonoturnadabaleia"[14]). It's also inhabited by the dog that guards the gates of hell: "I came to sniff bones with Hécuba. / The shame and humiliation is terrible" ("Eu vim farejar ossos com Hécuba. / É horrível a vergonha e a humilhação"). This is a dog who speaks in monologues, incessantly calling for the presence of an absent author, "missing the sky, the horizon." It lets people know that it does not snitch, does not spy on people, "it just sniffs whatever gets thrown its way."[15]

Its wandering leads through devastated lands; what emerges is a sense of waiting, an anticipation strictly without a horizon, but collective, nonetheless, choral: "with the rest of them / sweat beads / rolling down the head / heart beats faster / in the chest / when the bullet / skims the bucket / when the bombs explode / explode / they turn the bucket / to dust."[16] Voiceless, without words but "talking / talking / talking," producing a writing-in-tension that – inflected by some cultural manifestations of pre- and post-impeachment times – responds to the present moment with extraordinary vigor. And it places on us a comparable demand.

4
Negative Epiphanies

Three cultural interventions from 2019[1] call for a reflection on negative epiphany as a resource that repeatedly imposes itself on Brazilian artistic experience. Each one of these materializations is a different configuration of a similar kind of exposure: an exposure to the minefield constituted by the present moment in Brazil. All three stand as illuminations of this same minefield. Negative epiphanies, furthermore, seem to impose themselves on Brazilian art and culture especially when artistic experience wants to make evident both the materiality and corporeality of the world and the social nexus that gives dimension to this experience.

The examples I have in mind are not unique. What makes them stand out is their power of synthesis and their critical force, which positions them as counterpoints to both the nationalistic, *verde-amarelo* mystique and the ideological give-and-take that, in Brazil, had been signaling, throughout the 2010s, the emergence of a totalitarian cultural project (methodical but still ludicrous in its construction) linking a religious and moralist conservative turn (completely devoid of a self-reflexive dimension), a neo-fascist social media domination, and an authoritarian civil-military plan. The illuminations that emerge from the examples I have in mind here, in this reflection on epiphany, are critically articulated against this totalizing cultural project.

Let us begin with an "un-translation" Augusto de Campos titled "humanimais"[2] ("humanimals" – Figure 1). Campos published it in October 2019, using an Instagram account with the profile name "Poetamenos." In it, he is in dialogue with both e. e. cummings and with what the poem names as "soulless progress." The text is framed by large, virtual dollar signs (which bleed into the s's that appear as part of the text) and by a persistent green and yellow color story (an unmistakable allusion to the colors of the Brazilian flag). It's a set-up that appears elsewhere, in several other counter-poems of intervention published by Campos since the turn toward authoritarianism was consolidated in Brazil, following the impeachment of Dilma Rousseff.

"humanimais" grows increasingly yellow as it plays out on screen, in the same way that the inflatable duck campaign organized in 2015 by the FIESP (known as "Não Vou Pagar o Pato") grew more yellow – as yellow as the Brazilian soccer team shirts that became trademark symbols of the ultra-right marches and demonstrations that took place throughout Brazil around that time. In Campos' Instagram post, the patch of yellow starts small, covering nothing but the graphic space inside letters and the space inside punctuation marks and inside the letter "s." But it starts to expand at the end of the last line, and it ends up invading, significantly, entirely, an expression used to characterize the "band of humanimals," the same one used to conclude this un-translation – "soulless."

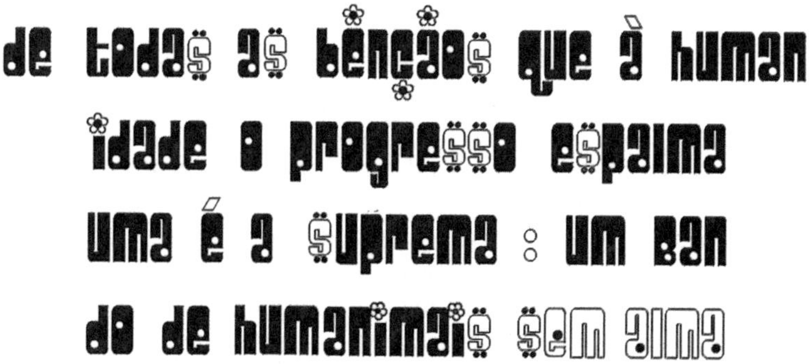

1 Black-and-white reproduction of "humanimais" (2019), a visual poem by Augusto de Campos published on October 15, 2016. The poem reads as follows: "among all the blessings progress brings to humanity, one reigns supreme: the band of soulless humanimals."

The second example I have in mind is a diptych by Cildo Meireles from the series titled "Eureka/Blindhotland" (published in "Mercado" – the business section of the *Folha de São Paulo* newspaper, on November 10, 2019), which can be read along the lines of Campos' poem, in the sense that it also exposes the blind spots of the political-economic logic of the authoritarian turn that took hold of Brazil over the course of the late 2010s.

Meireles' diptych[3] was deliberately placed in the (figurative, but sometimes real) minefield constituted by the business pages of a newspaper, and this made the diptych function, within the pages of the newspaper, in a way comparable to how his insertions into ideological circuits worked in the 1970s, when Meireles first enacted these insertions. Examples of them include "Projeto Coca-Cola," which consisted in labels placed on glass bottles of Coca-Cola displaying messages that ranged from political slogans ("Yankee Go Home") to instructions on how to turn glass soda bottles into Molotov cocktails. Also included in this series is "Projeto Cédulas," currency notes rubberstamped by the artist with messages such as "Quem matou Herzog?" ("Who Killed Herzog?") and placed back into circulation. The project was reactivated in 2017 and updated with language to reflect the political violence of the day: "Quem matou Marielle?" ("Who Killed Marielle?"), a reference to the assassination of Marielle Franco, the Brazilian politician, sociologist, feminist, and human rights activist brutally murdered on March 14, 2018.

The diptych published by Meireles in *Folha de São Paulo* on November 10, 2019, its silently ironic effect, can be easily overlooked by the more distracted segments of the newspaper's readership, and by those who can't be bothered to distinguish between the paper's reporting and its paid advertisements. It's a backward illustration of sorts, placed next to the usual mix of news and advertisements (an ad for Magazine Luiza, a Brazilian retail company, appears next to Meireles' intervention). For those who stop, even briefly, on the newspaper page where Meireles intervened, the critical–demonstrative effect that the artist achieved – from within, on the pages of the business section of the paper – is devastating.

Meireles' diptych would have worked well, losing none of its contrast, next to any item included in this section of the paper, the business section, which *Folha* tellingly designates as the "Market" pages, an expression that both underlines the financialization of the Brazilian economy, and also seems to have become a kind of omnipresent allegorical character ("the market") in political discussions and in the suppression of public policies throughout the nation. The artist himself arranged for the diptych to be placed in this section of the newspaper, where his work sets up an opposition between the concrete, slouching figure of a homeless person (a market "exclusion"), the ad for Magazine Luiza, and this whole section of the newspaper.

The photograph of the homeless person is pasted onto an image of one of the plastic balls featured in his series titled "Eureka/Blindhotland" (1970–5). In the 1975 exhibition with the same title (held at the Project Room of the Museum do Rio de Janeiro) and in subsequent installations, 200 identically sized balls are placed on the floor, each one with a different density and weight. The installation confronts viewers with, on the one hand, the appearance of equality and identity between the balls and, on the other hand, the shocking difference in their weight. The reappearance of these balls in the photograph included in the newspaper implodes the abstract logic with which a certain kind of economic reason acts "blindly," in the face of real life.

The third example of negative illumination I want to focus on comes from the world of theater, from *Macunaíma*, by Mário de Andrade, as staged by Bia Lessa and the Companhia Barca dos Corações Partidos, in a Rio de Janeiro run that concluded early in November 2019 (Figure 2). In this adaptation, epiphany may well reside in a certain intensity of discomfort. Some audience members who attended the play complained of a "lack of joy" in it, a sense of "darkness." It is as if, almost a century after the publication of Andrade's book (and in a context of increasingly clear threats against the environment and the survival of indigenous and minoritarian populations in the country), the predominantly nocturnal character of the book and of its last pages in particular (where a series of dissolutions are highlighted) could only now be perceived openly and clearly.

In Bia Lessa's theater adaptation of the book, negative illumination takes place on a deliberately darkened stage. As the image I reproduce here shows, the staging included an immense and very brief projection of a foreboding figure taken from German expressionist cinema. The theater of shadows thereby created lasts no more than a moment, and yet it isn't hard to recognize the nod it makes to F. W. Murnau's vampire in *Nosferatu* (1922).

2 Photograph by journalist Marília Soares Martins of Bia Lessa's theater adaptation of Mário de Andrade's *Macunaíma*.

The difference is that, whereas in Murnau's film shadows were projected onto a wall, in Lessa's staging of Andrade's book at the Teatro Carlos Gomes the light scheme is inverted, with dark curtains acting as a background and light taking up the space filled by shadows in Murnau's film.

This very large (and illuminated) figuration of shadows takes center stage at this point in the play, corresponding to the conclusion of Andrade's book. Mythical characters and apparitions, as well as any indication of a landscape, dissolve to the point of disappearing in this last segment of Andrade's narrative. The protagonist of the book, slowly losing his body, is included in this dissolution. The only thing that remains on stage in Bessa's adaptation is a huge poster on wheels reproducing the concluding final sentence of the rhapsody-novel: "Tem mais não" ("There's no more").

Let me move past these three examples to some observations regarding negative epiphany, mostly as it pertains to the sphere of Brazilian literary culture. I'll start with a previous reflection of mine that took place at the Centro de Pesquisa e Formação at the SESC, in São Paulo, toward the end of September 2018, before presidential elections were held in Brazil that year. I'll then turn to a series of counter-illuminations from Brazilian cultural production that are also in incisive dialogue with their context of production and their historical time.

Bliss, Epiphany, Intensity

My remarks on the negative epiphanic mode were delivered in a small colloquium titled "The Life of Literature: Bodies, Technologies, Happiness?" ("Vida da Literatura: corpos, tecnologias, felicidade?"). The starting point for the colloquium was a lecture by Hans Ulrich Gumbrecht in which he returned to issues that he had addressed during the last course he taught before he retired from Stanford University.

Gumbrecht focused on research related to a possible, constitutive relationship between literature and bliss, and he attempted to develop an understanding of Bliss beyond phenomena linked to individual life and to individual reading; instead, he focused his attention on a social dimension of that experience of "happiness." Aside from historically circumscribing the notions of literature and aesthetic experience during the first part of his presentation, Gumbrecht underlined the potential of certain texts and certain situations to increase palpability and presence, making way for an intensified perception of the body, of space, of the material world.

In the face of both the desire for, and the strictly particular aspect (inasmuch as it is also a phenomenon linked to individual existence) of, a shared social dimension (these are the conditions present in the notion of Bliss), the question that emerges thanks to the reflection offered by Gumbrecht is the following: is it possible for forms of community, for forms of social connection, to emerge in the context of moments of intensity, immersion, and ecstasy – the kind of moments that, from an existential perspective, are now seemingly expected from literary experience?

In the conversation that followed Gumbrecht's presentation, each interlocutor took a different approach. Alex Martoni tackled the notion of a "literary life" by considering an opposing concept, the death of art. Nicolau Spadani thematized soccer and returned to the radical notion of contingency that characterizes the sport itself. Guillerme Fóscolo focused his remarks on hybrid bodies (machine/organism), technopoesis, and the "life of technologies."

For my part, from the moment I found out what topic had been chosen for our discussion – and given the terms included in the title of the colloquium – I felt a certain unease with the task ahead of me. "Happiness" seemed almost unthinkable in a context of post-impeachment in Brazil, especially at that moment, when the electoral process clearly pointed to the growth of fascism in the country.

I envisioned my approach, then, as the flip side of the topic suggested by Gumbrecht. I focused on the pain (individual/collective) imbricated with the happiness and ecstasy potentially present in the experience of literature and art. All the while, I was conscious of the fact that the question mark next to the term "happiness" in the title of the colloquium already posed the term as a matter to be interrogated.

In his reflection on the notion of Bliss, Gumbrecht distinguishes this term from intensity (in his view, intensity is manifested in individual processes) and from epiphany (epiphany, he points out, lacks consistency, thickness, viscosity). It's worth pointing out, however, that in his *Production of Presence: What Meaning Cannot Convey* (2003), Gumbrecht highlights epiphany (as the appearance of something that requires space, something that Gumbrecht characterized as both present and absent) as an almost "intrusive" way of producing presence in and through language.

Gumbrecht points out that a "social dimension" can be glimpsed in Bliss as a "dimension of life" characterized by materiality, by contact, by substance (and not by form). In this sense, Bliss gets close to mystical ecstasy and to the Sanskrit notion of "Ananda," which suggests, precisely, the palpability and the taste of a thick fluid, a kind of syrup or honey. Moreover, there is a positivity inherent to the very notion of Bliss and the raptured experience of a state of ecstasy, the experience of feeling a strong sensation of belonging, of being inside, immersed, inhaling, ingesting.

I took as my point of departure some specific situations in the realm of Brazilian literary culture, situations where illuminations and moments of happiness and ecstasy are linked to strong negativity (sometimes to pain as well as to disgust). I sought out a kind of contrast, then, to the more nourishing, vital, and positive notion of Bliss, while attempting to preserve Bliss' corporeal and viscous aspects, its temporariness, its passage between perception and experience, and its vulnerability.

Before going down the path of negative epiphanies, it might be necessary to connect Gumbrecht's observations about literature and bliss both to Leo Spitzer's study of poetry and ecstasy and to Roland Barthes' essay on the pleasure of the text. Spitzer's thematizing of ecstasy in John Donne, San Juan de la Cruz, and Richard Wagner, and Barthes' opposition between *plaisir* and *jouissance*, will allow us to unfold the notional field linked to bliss. We will also focus on the public resonance of the oppressive–expiatory lubriciousness of police actions and of clandestine police organizations, as thematized in a text by Hélio Oiticica dated March 23, 1968, titled "The Hero-Antihero and the Anonymous Antihero" ("O herói anti-herói e o anti-herói anônimo"). This is especially fundamental when we consider the very hypothesis of a "social jouissance."

What Oiticica thematizes are the sacrificial persecutions that were unleashed not long before his text was written, the persecution of figures that had been depicted as "Public Enemy No. 1" by mainstream media and by the repressive apparatus of the Rio de Janeiro state government under the administration of Carlos Lacerda. Among those persecuted were "Mineirinho" (from Morro de Mangueira), "Micuçu" (from Morro de Babilônia), and "Cara de Cavalo" (from Favela do Esqueleto). "Mineirinho" was the subject of a *crônica*-requiem published by Clarice Lispector in *Revista Senhor* in 1962. The persecution of "Micuçu," on the other hand, was registered in "O ladrão de Babilônia" ("The Burglar of Babylon"), a poem by Elizabeth Bishop published in 1964. "Cara de Cavalo," on his part, was the subject of a homage produced by Hélio Oiticica in May 1966, *Bólide-Caixa No. 18-B33*, which features a reproduction of a newspaper photograph depicting the body of Cara de Cavalo, slain by more than 100 gun shots. Oiticica added the following caption to the photograph: "Aqui está e ficará! Contemplai seu silêncio heroico!" ("Here he is and here he will remain! Witness his heroic silence!").

In all these registers, what echoes is the question of a certain social thrill caused by these deaths, as well as the question of what authorizes, collectively, this level of violence. "While all this happened, we slept, we were (falsely) safe" ("Enquanto isso dormimos e falsamente nos salvamos"), Lispector wrote.[4] Here, it is imperative that we find out what social segments and what kind of lubricity is implicated in this group affinity for certain forms of lynching. It is also imperative that we seek out the possibility of a different response, endowed with epiphanic, self-revelatory force, and characterized, perhaps, by a different kind of joy, one that rejects extermination and homogenization, as Lispector herself suggests when she writes, in "Mineirinho": "Because I want to be the other" ("Porque eu quero ser o outro"). Furthermore, we must also investigate the possibility that this other kind of jouissance can, in fact, prove itself capable of collectively expanding the experience of literature and art.

Spitzer, Barthes, Oiticica

Let's return, by way of Leo Spitzer's "Three Poems on Ecstasy," to the notional field of intensity and ecstasy, keeping in mind, all the while, the structural, contrastive link both to persecutory-police lubricity and to the socially oppressive thrill that Hélio Oiticica writes about in "O herói anti-herói e o anti-herói anônimo." Let us also bear in mind the exemplarity in this regard of the Brazil of the Lava-Jato and the post-Lava-Jato era – the Brazil of digital and media lynchings, of virulent police actions in different parts of urban peripheries, of armed groups operating in indigenous territories in several parts of the country with the intention of making non-viable collective forms of owning and working the land. A series of negative epiphanies carrying transformative, self-revelatory potential emerges, antagonistically, from this ecstatic–persecutory field, a series that includes works like those recently produced by Augusto de Campos, Cildo Meireles, and Bia Lessa.

The fundamental element in Spitzer's essay is the comparatist perspective. If, on the one hand, what this essay presents are forms of thematization and poetic configuration of ecstasy, forms of the "union of the human with something outside of it" – if every analytic segment in the essay is comprised of a focused engagement with a particular body of work, they all end up pointing to a contrastive field. This field frames for us the mystical union of two souls that turn into one: the atemporal allegory in Donne; the spiritual experience that turns into "adventurous demand" guided by the night, by the "force of flesh and time," in San Juan de la Cruz' poetry; the dynamism of the dissolution, the self-annihilation, the ecstasy of death, of Tristan and Isolde in Wagner.

In the contrast Barthes sets up between pleasure and jouissance, what matters is the hesitation operating in the incessant call for another expression, in a regime of potential variation. In Gumbrecht's remarks – and not gratuitously – the expression "Bliss" comes hand in hand with constant incursions by other, possible, closely related and diverse terms – intensity, epiphany, Ananda. This "margin of indecision" is also present in the negative illuminations that forcefully appear in Brazilian literary experience; this, too, is not gratuitous.

Near the beginning of Barthes' essay, the reader is presented with the following caveat: "Pleasure/Bliss: terminologically, there is always a vacillation – I stumble, I err. In any case, there will always be a margin of indecision; the distinction will not be the source of absolute classifications, the paradigm will falter, the meaning will be precarious, revocable, reversible, the discourse incomplete."[5] This indecision gained supplementary force in Jacó Guinsburg's Portuguese translation of Barthes' text, as we can see in a note Guinsburg included to justify his choice of the word *fruição* to render, in Portuguese, the meaning of "jouissance." The note also includes a deliberately long list of almost-synonyms: *gozo / prazer físico / fruição / posse / usufruto*. He writes:

> Some critics think that the best translation of *jouissance* to Portuguese is *gozo*, to the extent that this work captures, in a more explicit way, the sense of physical pleasure inherent to the term in French. On our part, we believe that the word *fruição* (enjoyment, fruition), though more delicate, conveys the same meaning, and it has the advantage of reproducing, poetically, the phonetic movement of the French term. In any case, the reader will find here all the pleasure he sets out to enjoy.[6]

In Richard Miller's translation to English, published by Farrar, Straus, and Giroux in 1975, a similar dilemma emerged, and his proposal to translate *jouissance* as "bliss" was praised by Richard Howard in the introduction to the volume. Howard, however, also noted that, in truth, another term, more crude ("to come," "coming") would have been evidently more precise. The Portuguese word *gozo* manages to capture this sense of the term.

"The Story of 'Bliss,' Annotated"

If we follow the trail left behind by these hesitations, and keeping in mind Gumbrecht's observations about Bliss, anyone who turns to contemporary Brazilian literature will inevitably and almost immediately think of Ana Cristina Cesar when reflecting on the conceptualization of Bliss. One text in particular will come to mind, "O conto 'Bliss' anotado," which takes on Katherine Mansfield's short story titled "Bliss," and which includes a long discussion by the Brazilian poet on matters related to her translation of the short story, a discussion Cesar synthesizes in 90 explanatory notes.

The term "bliss" in that story plays a curious role, one that Ana Cristina Cesar did not entirely resolve in her translation. For while the translation renders "Bliss" as *êxtase* (contrary to the previous, 1940 translation of the short story, by Érico Verissimo, which opted for the term *felicidade*), and while, therefore, Ana's version chooses a particular formula for her Portuguese translation, she also leaves the English word as is, including it in her text (on the title page, for instance). She thus opts for a kind of non-substitution as part of the translation process.

Commenting on the translation, Ana Cristina Cesar writes: "The translation of the title deserves special attention. There is no equivalent for 'bliss' in Portuguese. Dictionaries offer some words with approximately the same meaning: *felicidade*, *alegria*, *satisfação*, *contentamento*, *bem-aventurança*, etc. I chose the word *êxtase*, because it expresses an emotion that either goes beyond what the word 'happiness' captures, or that is stronger than it."[7] And there is another side to this, something other than the difficulties inherent to literal translation, something that speaks to a fundamental aspect of Mansfield's story, something that seems to explain much of Ana's interest in the story. Bliss in this story is painful. It is an intense moment; it moves from a sensation of euphoria, quasi-ecstatic, to disappointment, to an abyss – a person momentarily at her peak, then suddenly falling, falling hopelessly, her state of rapture disappearing completely.

There's a tension here between rapture and pain, and there is also the physical dimension of those high points of ecstasy, all of which are underlined several times throughout the short story. Bodies touch each other in the narrative; it captures the delightful physical proximity of two female bodies. "What was there in the touch of that cool arm that could fan – fan – start blazing – blazing – the fire of bliss that Bertha did not know what to do with?"[8]

There is also a garden in Mansfield's text, along with a very strong sensorial dimension throughout the story, something that evidently interested Ana Cristina Cesar, the translator, as a possible way of thinking the body and feminine sensibility (as well as relationships marked by intense affect and almost unspeakable extremes) through literature. She closely observes Mansfield's narrative construction of these intensities, and there are echoes of that imagetic unfolding in a well-known poem by Cesar included in her posthumous book *Inéditos e dispersos* (1985),[9] which features a lookout, light, and simultaneity as signs of an erotic-ecstatic event.

Light breaks.
We arrived at the same time to the lookout
Where light always breaks.
At the same time we say some
thing.
Then I fall curving
downwards, I come back and shine.
Extreme lookout, a place to come.

The poem is basically a self-explanatory description of the experience of bliss. It works without the conceit of simile. In Mansfield's story, when it captures a sensation as experienced by Bertha Young – "a feeling of bliss – absolute bliss! – as though you'd suddenly swallowed a bright piece of that late afternoon sun and it burned in your bosom"[10] – what we have is a description of the ecstatic state and, nonetheless, it is as if that description was impossible, hence the expression "as though." In César's poem, there is no "as if" – there is a lookout, light, and there is also just the positivity of rapture, with no pain, but with a clear indication of the violence inherent to ecstasy.

Cesar learned to detect violence in those states of rapture thanks to her perceptive reading of Christopher Isherwood, and thanks, as well, to both some comments by Isherwood transcribed by his biographer, Paul Piazza, in *Christopher Isherwood: Myth and Anti-Myth* (1978), and to some remarks by Piazza himself regarding *A Single Man* (1962). Not only did

Cesar find in Isherwood the notion of ecstasy in its relation to bliss; she also learned that the expression "bliss" was not all that common in English, and that, when used, this expression was generally linked to the world of homosexual relationships, where the intensity of transgression would be such that, more than a simply pleasant kind of happiness, what was necessary was the idea of Bliss, in order to highlight another kind of intensity, with different scales of violence and (orgasmic) spasm.

Citing Isherwood, Cesar writes: "An interesting quote by C. Isherwood establishes a difference between bliss and plain happiness. The narrator feels that the term 'happiness' is closer to heterosexual relationships, while bliss, which is more violent and 'sensational' and not just a feeling of happiness, is that which a person looks for in homosexual relations (something not properly of this world?)."[11] Reading Isherwood led Cesar to eroticize her own work as a translator (she went on to construct, in her notes, an erotics of translation) and this, of course, prevents her from keeping the word *felicidade* – the word used by Érico Veríssimo – in her own translation of "Bliss." What's missing from that word is the ability to designate a state of violence where one feels, and is, beyond oneself, a state in which we can absorb things from others. It is as if happiness was something to be kept private, with ecstasy, on the other hand, as something characterized by an intense motion toward an outside. This, in turn, is related to Gumbrecht's remarks on a certain form of (imagined) sociability linked to states of Bliss.

In Mansfield's fiction, aside from those ecstatic moments where the narrative movement thickens and gains viscosity and ineffability, we can also detect, in her literary method, a peculiar taste for epiphanic moments, when imagetic condensations (as well as condensations of intensity) materialize, interrupting the flow of the story. Instead of narrative flow, strange images emerge, illuminations, until the narration returns but now with a different dimension that results from these interruptions, these figural breaks constructed inside the story. What's peculiar about this is that, very frequently, this movement of figural condensation and of momentary interruption of the flow of the story comes hand in hand with some negativity or other, because this excess, this ecstasy, is simultaneously an ecstasy of pain. It is not a joyful thing; it is an excess of pain.

In this sense, it is worth remembering another well-known short story by Mansfield, "The Fly" (1922), where she describes a fly inside an ink well, drowning in ink and left there to drown, taken out only toward the end of the story, right before it dies. In truth, the story hints at a certain kind of cruelty linked to the writing process; agony, as portrayed in the story, is also an epiphany regarding the process of writing: a negative epiphany. Some of the key elements of Ana Cristina César's comments on "Bliss" (and of the echoes of Mansfield's writings in César's own poetry) concern fluctuations in tone, moments of rapture, and a dimension of pain that inhabits them. Furthermore, it isn't difficult to sense a certain trace of Mansfield's epiphanies in Lispector's own epiphanies (Lispector, too, was a Mansfield reader), especially those with greater physicality and with a negative dimension.

Instante-Já

We may or may not agree with João Camillo Penna when he reads (in "O nu de Clarice Lispector"[12]) the transformation at the heart of the epiphanic moment as the key to explaining all her work and, at the same time, perhaps as one of the biggest commonplaces in the scholarship on Lispector. Regardless of how we feel about this, Lispector's appropriation of epiphany is nonetheless significant and has noticeable specificities. It functions, in her work, as a movement between revelation and disgust, between the imaginary and everyday life. It also functions as a kind of an anti-bliss, but full of viscosity, of corporeality, and of vital potential.

In this sense, Lispector's dialogue with Mansfield's work becomes even more evident. The impact Mansfield's diaries and short stories had on Lispector is well known. She herself underlined it in interviews and in conversations with friends. In "Mistério desentranhado," published in *Clarice Lispector com a ponta dos dedos* (2005), Vilma Arêas draws attention to affinities and differences between the two writers. She highlights, particularly, Lispector's decisive dialogue with Mansfield's fiction in the composition of short stories such as "Mensagem" and "Mistério em São Cristóvão."

Bliss as it relates to Brazilian literature seems to entail a negative configuration, especially as a space that allows for movement between individual writing and the weight of the world. Considering that conceptual zone that includes the notion of Bliss (which I linked to moments of body contact, of extreme sensations, of illumination; to epiphanic interventions; to pain and negativity), a revision of the notions both of the *instante-já* (Lispector's "instant-now") and of Manuel Bandeira's *alumbramento* ("illumination") seems necessary.

Lispector's remarks in *Água Viva* (1973) – on her quest to find the "fourth dimension of the instant-now,"[13] on her inquiry into "matter made sensitive by the chill of the instant," on her investigation of "instants of metamorphosis" and the "terrible beauty" of "their sequence and concomitance" – are shaped by a kind of conventional, epiphanic meter. It's worth nothing, however, that it is through disgust, through the sudden awareness of alterity, through the tension related to social place itself, that some of the most relevant fictional illuminations are constructed. They seem very distant from a certain ineffability that tends to characterize the literary use of epiphany; their poetic measure is a different one. They operate, these negative epiphanies, as counter-illuminations.

We see this in a short story like "Amor,"[14] generally considered prototypical of the epiphanic in the work of Lispector. The sight of a "blind man chewing gum" as seen by Ana, one of the story's characters, does not stay within the confines of revelation, because this man, his gum chewing, seems to insult her, and at the same time she suffocates with feelings of pity and nausea. What's first taken in through the eyes starts to take over her entire body; the perception of the world intensifies, it turns into keenness, into goosebumps, and all the while the world becomes exposed, in all its rawness.

Something similar happens, as is well known, with *The Passion According to G. H.* (1964). Smells appear in the story, an estrangement vis-à-vis the absent housekeeper, and there is also a breaking of limits: the eating, the incorporation of the radically othered body of an insect. If viscosity grounds the rapture of that moment, on the flip side of G. H., this is evidently nothing like the "syrup" evoked by Gumbrecht in his talk at the SESC colloquium. In Lispector's text, we are in the realm of disgust, of nausea, of the slime where the roach lives. What remains, though, is fluidity, thickness, the possibility of eating, of swallowing.

In this sense, we can think of *The Passion According to G. H.* as the construction of a moment of bliss and of actual ecstasy, beyond the simply epiphanic. This follows from the contact with that slime, the slime of the roach G. H. swallows, which, in truth, exposes a process of recognizing the other, that poor other, the one corresponding to the maid's quarters. Here, the moment of bliss (epiphany as contradiction, as negation, as revelation of the limits of the world, as revelation of the place of class and race) functions as a path toward an outside of the self, like the one Lispector invokes in her text on Mineirinho.

These negative epiphanies, which threaten to become the sensation of bliss, usually involve the hypothesis of the subject going beyond itself in the direction of another that defines it. In Lispector, this process explicitly involves the body, chewing (also present in "Amor"), and swallowing, eating. What we have here is a literal tasting of the other, an eating of the other, a "wanting to be the other." This stands in sensible opposition to the "discourse of 'them'" (as thematized by Luiz Eduardo Soares in *O Brasil e seu duplo*, 2019),[15] a discourse where alterity and extermination are usually conjugated, the way they are in Brazil, in relation to indigenous populations and peripheral communities, in relation to women, to poor people, to Black Brazilians, and to LGBTQI+ people.

"Alumbramento"

We find in Manuel Bandeira a similar movement toward ordinary life, toward the other, not just in his way of understanding the notion of "illumination," but also in some of his epiphanic inverses. In "A Beleza humilde é áspera," Davi Arrigucci summarizes the notion of illumination in Bandeira's work as follows:

> In the plane of irradiation of modern art in Brazil, especially in its historical modernist moment [...], Bandeira reveals, early on, the subtle antennas he possessed, the ones he kept refining in order to capture a diffuse form of poetry in the world of small things, the world of everyday things, gathering elements from different contexts. He learned how to regard these things, getting closer to matters that had not, until then, been considered poetic. This poetry could emerge unexpectedly, in a sudden illumination, as he called that moment of

> inspiration or elucidation: an outbreak of elevated emotion, which could manifest itself in rare moments anywhere, always demanding from the poet an attitude of passionate listening.[16]

Instants of illumination and revelation, exemplified in the vision of a naked woman in the poem titled "Alumbramento," generally involve this passionate kind of listening. They demand close attention as well as the poetic affirmation of some "small nothings" from everyday life. There are also, on the other hand, in the work of Bandeira, illuminations of a different sort. If, in "Alumbramento," there is a very violent positivity in the vision of a woman's nudity – "I saw the heavens! I saw the heavens," "I saw her naked!" – something different happens, for instance, in a poem such as "O Bicho" ("The Creature"), from 1947. The photos of homeless people Cildo Meireles included in "Eureka/Blindhotland," which I mentioned earlier, approximate, in a way, the somber revelation constructed by Bandeira in this poem:

> Yesterday I saw a creature
> amidst the garbage in the courtyard,
> hunting for food amidst the debris.
>
> When it found something
> it didn't look or smell
> – just wolfed it down.
> The creature wasn't a dog
> or a cat
> or a rat.
>
> The creature, my God, was a man.[17]

Brazil's structural inequities echoed and continue to echo in "O Bicho." In it, we find a negative illumination, an internal process of self-correcting perception, wherein the very definition of the human is modified. Simultaneously, the poem makes way for the duration of an instant of illumination, expanding its reach and its critical dimension. The intimate universe that provides, in the poem, a vision of an inner courtyard is crossed by misery and by the hunger of a creature that the poem hesitates to call a man, because he appears to lack minimal conditions of subsistence. And yet the fundamental movement of the poem is precisely the affirmation of humanity, by way of the very redefinition of man when confronted with an Other, to a creature glanced almost unintentionally close to home.

These examples from Lispector and Bandeira could be expanded to include a great number of negative illuminations found in modern and contemporary Brazilian literature. Drummond de Andrade's "A Máquina do Mundo" (1951) could be added to this list, and so could Oswald de Andrade's *O Rei da Vela* (1933), with its crude exposition of the economic nexus at the heart of inequity in Brazil. *Grande Sertão: Veredas* (1956) by Guimarães Rosas could also be included, given the painful epiphany that emerges at the sight of the dead, female, naked body of the *jagunço* Reinaldo/Diadorim. Perhaps it is possible to take the examples I discussed here as paradigmatic of the negative trace that can be found in the epiphanies characteristic of modern and contemporary Brazilian literature. This same trace can be found in processes of condensation and awareness (they emerge as illumination) where the visualization of the world takes place not as acceptance, as communion, as positivity, but as the materialization of a self-revealing experience tied to violent negation.

If we go back to Bia Lessa's work – not to her *Macunaíma*, but to her 2017 staging of *Grande Sertão: Veredas* – and if we turn specifically to the moment when Riobaldo sees a dead Diadorim, the moment when he sees his female body for the first time, it is significant that this negative illumination became one of the main objects of discussion in articles published after Lessa's theatrical creation. The question at the time was formulated as a question of whether the exhibition of the physical, naked body in Lessa's staging was not, perhaps, too obvious, given that most audience members were familiar with the ending of this romance, and given, too, that readers and audience members were aware that Reinaldo and Diadorim were in fact the same person.

Lessa anticipated this problem and deployed a kind of double presence of the body: one ghostly (using cut-outs from a photographic image of the nude body of the lead actress) and one real (the actual nude body of the actress) in her theatricalization of the text. Her approach yielded a body that appeared onstage, but cut and pasted, in a two-dimensional format that looked deliberately precarious, blurry. The image remains visible throughout, but the negative force of Riobaldo's sighting of Diadorim imposed itself as a material presence, demanding a corporeal dimension. This is the reason why Lessa eventually did without the photographic cut-outs and opted for the actress in the play (Luiza Lemmertz) to remain onstage in the final moments. The sight of that dirty, nude body, that negative illumination, seems to pulsate amid a great heap of dead bodies (some real, represented by actors on stage; some made of felt), its mass swollen by the dark, abandoned clothing shared by the group of characters in the play.

These revealing situations, these negative epiphanies, impose, in a way, a physicality, an intrusion, one that is generally proportional to their potential to reveal and transform perception. A physicality that is proportional, too, to their exposure of the viscous, of the hard consistency of the joyful/sorrowful experience of the world. And if these manifestations are intensified by means of "subitaneidade" ("suddenness"), by the irruption of an outside, the physicality that is inherent to them underlines a virtual deindividuation, through the intensified consciousness of the presence of the world. That world is physical, and so are the bodies and the things that impose themselves on that world.

Examples of this include the sighting of the dead, nude body of Reinaldo/Diadorim; Arandir's dead body, lying on the street, in *O beijo no asfalto* (1961) by Nelson Rodrigues; the dead bull in Bandeira's poems; Miguel Rio Branco's photograph of a dead dog; and Nuno Ramo's *Monólogo para um cachorro morto*. By way of contrast, in a vibrating, fragile, but still lively movement, we can think of the insect trapped in light in Drummond's "A Bruxa." We can also think of the blowfly buzzing around the trash in the poem "Limiar" by Carlito Azevedo. And – again and again – we can think of the man living in inhumane conditions in Bandeira's "O Bicho."

This negative path to epiphany became characteristic of literature and the artistic culture produced in Brazil after modernism. It seems, however, that it has been enacted with particular fervor in different dystopic contexts, such as the 21 years of dictatorship in Brazil as well as the rise of the ultra-right movements and conservative demands of all sorts that took hold of everyday life in Brazil before and after the impeachment of Dilma Rousseff. A compelling example of this enactment is the revelatory force found in the poetry of Francisco Alvim, which dates to the decades of military authoritarianism in Brazil. It exposed, in small cuts, the social links (generally implicit) that sustained and continue to sustain Brazilian conservatism. Another example

– a paradigmatic one – is the immense anthill Antonio Callado places dead in the middle of Brazil in his book *Quarup* (1967), an epiphanic-dystopic figuration revisited by Kleber Mendonça Filho toward the end of his film *Aquarius* (2016), where the filmmaker seems to be exposing the potential anti-democratic dissolution menacing the present moment.

In her translation of Mansfield's "Bliss," Ana Cristina Cesar subjected the fierce and painful process of illumination to a beautiful process of conceptualization. That this process took place just before the last years of the military dictatorship in Brazil is hardly a coincidence. In this sense, it's worth returning to the poem I discussed in chapter 3 of this book ("Artistic Actions / Political Actions"),[18] a poem that, in my view, performed a similar function in relation to the recent history of Brazil.

Originally published without a title, and marked above all by its date, the Angelica Freitas omen-poem I have in mind here is, in part, a dialogue with a photo by Caco Argemi published by the newspaper *Zero Hora* on May 14, 2016. It shows mounted police, their horses pursuing teachers and public employees in Porto Alegre. It is also a configuration – somewhat in slow motion – of a negative epiphany, not just for the lyrical subject of the poem, but for anyone who could perceive what was going on (not everyone could; some were slow to grasp the intensity of what was happening in Brazil). Freita's poem is therefore almost a description from the outside, until the moment the world enters – not through television, but sensorially – into the realm of that private world. And at that moment, the poem changes direction.

Considering the speed of implementation of a project designed to dissolve democratic institutions in Brazil, the silence in the mainstream media about the economic nexus of an expanded fascist movement, and the increased lethal virulence of the police, perhaps the negativity expressed in Angélica Freitas' poem could be seen, three years later, not as a premonition but as astonishment in the face of what was already there.

Fright of the Day

It's worth examining, in this context, the work of two of the most important Brazilian contemporary poets, Augusto de Campos and Carlito Azevedo, who have cultivated strong counter-illuminations and a methodical dialogue with the path these negativities entail, evident in their process of composition, which is characterized by the precision with which temporal observation is exposed, by the precision with which the present is registered. Each of them proceeds, however, following their own, particular poetic diction.

Carlito Azevedo seems to go in the direction of counter-illumination in "A maldição de Adão,"[19] a text that, according to the poet, might end up having a different name, or might become part of a longer poem. In it, Azevedo, who regularly works with the construction of counter-illuminations, is in dialogue with negative epiphanies he has rehearsed in recent years.

If, in "Livro do cão" ("Book of the Dog," 2016[20]), for instance, the path-poem, the search for the author, is narrated by a dying dog, the more recent poem ("A maldição de Adão") is constructed from the perspective of a subject-on-the-run. In "Livro do cão," the length of the poem amplifies the very process of agony, much like Mansfield's "The Fly" intensifies the death of a fly in an inkwell. In "A maldição de Adão," the cine-poetic aspect of the poem (achieved even though the poem is entirely verbal), its images-in-passing, its movement, impede, strike through, and blur the epiphanic that emerges here and there in the poem. Another text by Azevedo, from 1991, proceeds in much the same way, and it also opens with a focus on landscape not unlike the opening of "A maldição de Adão." Notice, in this sense, the poem titled "Limiar" ("Threshold") from the book *Collapsus Linguae* (1991). It, too, is a negative epiphany:

> The milky way is tousled.
> Bodies expended against the light.
> With no artifice, the mountain
> kindles its smudge on the beach.
> The trashcan on the corner is
> the last launching pad for the fly's last flight
> against a convulsive century.[21]

In it, we witness not just a hint of a landscape contour (an outline of Rio de Janeiro, signaled by a mountain and beaches), but also a description of changes in luminosity and a site in transition. It isn't just the century that's convulsive here; it's the whole scene: the sky, the geography, the bodies spent against the light. We also witness a passage from a description of a briefly experienced (and potentially beautiful) natural sight (Pão de Açucar mountain, itself undergoing transformations) to the register of a diminished environment (trash, flies) that dismantles this sight, against an intentionally disproportional temporal background ("a convulsive century").

In "A maldição de Adão," we also find a description that breaks apart, a description of marine scenery dominated by the sight of a lit-up shipyard:

> It was pretty, seeing
> at night
> from the window, at home,
> or from the wall
> of Praia 55
> the shipyard
> wrapped in its
> own lights
> overlapping,
> welders, torches,
> reflectors, spotlights,
> pendant lights,
> flashovers,
> lighting
> but no
> storm.[22]

This is a landscape before any kind of storm, lighting notwithstanding, a landscape of gazes that cross each other during the workers' shift change at the shipyards – mute signs of potential revolt, a revolution that the poet borrows as a potential hypothesis for the poem. Constructed with a cinematographic method (cuts are what adds movement to it), the poem moves forward and back; and, amidst the frights of a day, it returns to a here and now. Everything happens in a moment: "a hand, frozen, on a door knob." The poem situates itself in the here and now of a head exploding with pain, of an "uber driver out there / wailing / oppressed," of "all the voices of the multitude / emanating / from the heart of darkness."

The painful vision of these frightful things leads, in a way, to a textual sequence composed in the manner of a kind of anti-Angelus Novus. Like the Angelus, this sequence also comes from "the kingdom of grief and of tragedy":

> Someone that you've
> never seen
> runs desperately
> toward you
> someone or some
> apparition from the kingdom
> of grief and of tragedy;
> someone like an
> antagonistic contradiction
> in a sea of
> non-antagonistic
> contradictions;
> someone drowning
> in the mystic trifles
> of the street at dusk;
> someone whose
> brain sponges
> would never truss
> the unassailable foundations
> of a solid empire;
> someone who needs
> to talk to you
> at any cost;
> but you're so absent minded
> you enter your car
> or the movie theater
> or the elevator
> you get away without even
> knowing that you're getting away
> from the whirlpool
> at the bottom
> of the witch's
> cauldron
> of history.[23]

There is a visible transit, in these poems, between, on the one hand, expressions/states such as bliss, enlightenment, and the instant-now and, on the other hand, a movement in the direction of negative epiphanies that impose a critical self-awareness on Brazilian literary writing (a self-awareness that moves beyond the sphere of literature, exposing the urgent need for self-revealing and for transformative illumination in dystopian contexts). It is significant, in this sense, that in "A maldição de Adão" the (vanishing) question seems to be about what to do (and where to go) in the face of the here and now.

A poem by Augusto de Campos titled "Profilograma: Duchamp" (published on his Instagram account in 2019) poses a similar question (Figure 3). The answer, in Campos' poem, is *eu re/spiro*. Campos here explicitly plays with Duchamp's notion of the *inframince*: vomit, ejaculation, blowing one's nose, snoring, piss, tears, passing out, whistling, spitting, singing, sighs.[24] He also echoes the well-known Duchampian mantra, "I like living, breathing better than working."[25] In Campos' poem, breathing functions as "a work that isn't inscribed anywhere."

A more immediate question arises: "what to do?" The answer operates, in Augusto's poem, with the reduction and scansion – "//respiro-re/spiro//" – of Duchamp's observation about living, breathing, and working. Furthermore, in an almost inevitable echo of our political and artistic imaginary, the poem juxtaposes a quite commonplace question ("and what / are / you / doing / now / ?") both to Lenin's paradigmatic title-question (What is to

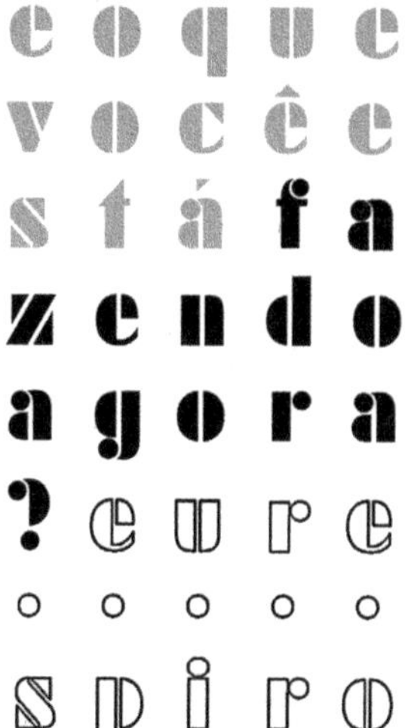

3 Black-and-white reproduction of "Profilograma: Duchamp" by Augusto de Campos.

be done?) and to Duchamp's rejection of the conventional idea of a work of art.

Faced with the present juncture, the emphasis on the question "what are we supposed to do?," the echo of Lenin's question (with its inherent demand for an articulation between theory and praxis), and the emphasis on Duchamp's projects and notes all seem to add to the scansion in Campos' poem (*eu re/spiro*), and to the antithetical (but homophonic) play between *respiro/expiro* ("I breathe / I die"), adding a speculative–operational dimension to that sense of breathing.

In "A maldição de Adão," what's most prevalent is vertigo, as well as a subject on the run, harassed by frightful sights. The poem also features a car, a movie theater, and an elevator used by the subject to escape, with no awareness of the whirlpool pulling him down to the bottom of the cauldron. There is someone running desperately in the poem, in the direction of this subject. It is impossible not to perceive, in this section of Azevedo's poem – in this quasi-encounter between someone marching forward unstoppably and "someone whose / brain sponges / would never truss / the unassailable foundations / of a solid empire" – a reference to Benjamin's well-known remarks on Klee.

The image here points to Azevedo's extended textual series on angels, as well as to Benjamin's commentary on the angel of history, in his text titled "On the Concept of History," and to the Angelus Novus in Paul Klee's 1920s watercolor (the same angel Benjamin read as a figure wanting to move away from something, something it stares at intently, something it perceives as catastrophe – the continuum of history – while ruins gather at his feet, piled sky high).

As Benjamin writes, describing Klee's work, this angel would like to stop to wake up the dead from their slumber, to recompose fragments, to invoke the vanquished, but a storm pushes him forward, irreversibly; the angel faces away from the storm while the pile of ruins grows taller. And if, in Benjamin's reflection, it is the angel who reveals to us the catastrophic logic of progress, in Carlito Azevedo's poem the figure running desperately in the direction of the subject-on-the-run is the one who reveals to him, in a critical illumination, the possibility of escaping (without even knowing he's escaping, as the poem suggests) from the whirlpool, from the cauldron of the spells of history.

In Azevedo's poem, if the catastrophic plot is found over there, far away, the wreck, the dead, and the vanquished run in the direction of the figure running away in a car, in an elevator. Contrary to the devastating storm critically figured as an image of progress by Benjamin, we may note the presence of another idea of a storm toward the end of Azevedo's poem. It's a storm with thunder and lightning but not quite a storm – an exchange of glances but not quite a rebellion. And yet it is also a premonition, borrowed, cinematographically, from the past: a premonition of a potential revolt. What we have here is an interpellation – present and pending – from apparitions hailing from "the kingdom of grief and of tragedy" and from the "suffering of those who pay the price of history."[26]

5

Critical Grammars of the Middle Classes: Observations on the Narrative Fictions of André Sant'Anna, Veronica Stigger, and Vilma Arêas (and on Some Other Literary Methods of Confrontation)

In "The Suicide of the Middle Classes," a text included in her book *Les années 10* (2014),[1] French poet Nathalie Quintane pursues a brief and sharp investigation of the middle classes. Two years later, she transformed her inquiry into a question – *What Is to Be Done about the Middle Classes?*[2] – and the question, in turn, morphed into an entire book. The topic seems just as pressing, and just as urgent, when confronting the evident dissolution of solidarity and the increasingly anti-democratic character evinced in recent years by the middle classes in Brazil. The 2018 election results are far from the only sign of this dissolution; we can see it in the intense support a significant portion of the middle classes showed for policies in favor of restricting freedom of expression, curtailing civil and workers' rights, and expanding the militarization both of public spaces and of hubs of political activity throughout the nation.

Quintane's earlier essay concludes with the following suggestion: in order to confront the decisive issue – the social issue – underpinning the actions of the middle classes, perhaps what is necessary is to undertake, somehow, a purge of categories (in the name of "personal hygiene," as the poet emphasized).

This entails setting aside exclusively classificatory polls as well as indicators related to income, education, profession, values, net worth, housing, and lifestyle, the kind of indicators used to define a middle class. We could opt, instead, for a self-reflective movement – two fingers down one's throat, as the poet suggests, to gag oneself into a good purge – the result of which would go beyond categories, moving into scatologically literal territory. Something like a vomiting of the self.

Key to these efforts, in Quintane's view, is to unfold our attention (focused as it usually is on quantitative data) in a way that allows us to direct it toward things that cling to our very entrails – "our" entrails, to the extent that we, too, belong to the middle classes. Attention redirected in this way would also land on the values and hierarchies, the fears of social disqualification and cultural discrediting, that we should be visualizing internally, as constitutive elements of our sensibility, imbricated in our most banal choices. In this sense, Quintane suggests, thinking about the middle classes requires vomiting the self out of ourselves, first and foremost.

Fingers Down the Throat

This critical, self-inclusive perspective is a distinctive aspect of some of the best exercises in fiction in Brazilian literature from the first decades of the twenty-first century. Highlights from this period include the series of diatribes by "upstanding citizens" systemically elaborated by André Sant' Anna since the publication of his short novel *Sexo*, and the stories included in *Sexo e amizade* (2007). Also in that group are the situations of imminent conflict and the thorough visualization of class frameworks completed by Vilma Arêas in very short stories such as the two versions of "Na rua" and in the series of "snapshots" included in *Um beijo por mês* (2018).[3] Veronica Stigger's conversation fragments, commonplace phrases, and invented canned expressions as compiled in *Delírio de damasco* can also be added to that group. Her cruel fictionalizations,[4] constructed with calculated irony – and exemplified by stories such as "Os anões," "Tristeza e Isidoro," "Festa de casamento," "Mancha" – are especially good examples of the kind of literature I have in mind here.

Let me set aside, for the moment, the work of Sant' Anna, Stigger, and Arêas, and spend some time with a group of authors frequently labeled "cruel," whose work finds resonance in the distinct methods of these three writers. The cruelty that reverberates in these works is usually linked not just to specific topics or ways of constructing plot lines, but also, and especially, to its potential to expose and criticize networks of power (corresponding to narrative structures and to the literary use of language), culturally rooted (and generally tacit) forms of legitimizing social inequality, racial and gender exclusions, and the self-recognition of the middle classes.

The "cruelty" usually associated with these texts is fundamentally constituted by constraints imposed on readers (especially when these readers belong to the middle classes, or when they subscribe to middle-class values) by the activation of mechanisms that potentially destabilize the usually invisible grammars of legitimation exposed by that very literature. At times, these texts function in a cruelly self-inclusive way, as suggested by the image of "fingers down the throat" crafted by Quintane when she writes about a "suicide of the middle class."

Let´s keep, then, the three more recent authors highlighted here as a kind of vanishing point. And before we return to each of them, to each of their literary methods, let's take a few steps back, focusing on writers who are distinctly present in the work of these authors. In this sense, it's worth recalling, to start with, the work of the playwright Nelson Rodrigues, his indirect constructions which rely on ready-made phrases, pseudo-verbal reasonings, and exacerbated commonplaces, and his more evident and explicitly designated forms of the chorus. Perhaps it's also worth returning to the work of other authors such as Dalton Trevisan and his mechanics of the cliché; to the Clarice Lispector of both *The Hour of the Star* (1977) and her short fictions that wear "cruelty as a crown" (for example, the whole book *The Via Crucis of the Body*); and to the "polymorphous voices" of Alvim's poetry, which configure, as Roberto Schwarz has observed, "something like a fragmentary national comedy, interior and exterior."[5]

We find in the work of these authors an intensified attention to the operations that expose the political dimension of language and literature. Their work develops a critical kind of listening, attentive to the forms power takes when it makes itself heard and to the "discourse of arrogance" that Roland Barthes underlined in his inaugural lecture at the Collège de France.[6] This is a kind of listening that makes explicit the assertive structures, stereotypes, moralities, hierarchies, classifications, the forms of subservience, and the forced exclusions that inhabit both language and literary culture.

This kind of listening also makes explicit concomitant or stealthy movements of blockage and transformation, as seen, for example, in the irruption of screams and inarticulate voices in Rodrigues' *Álbum de família* (*Family Album*, 1946). These writings dramatize the sedimentation that structures them, and they expose, in literary language, prosodic, syntactical, and semantic traces of social organization, as well as the exclusions that constitute these forms of organization. They also point not just to what links together, what sediments, but also to the tensions that guide this collective sense of scale.

The capacity to articulate this collective scale (and to expose the power structures that operate in language and in social organization) with complex forms of writing is what makes the work of Rodrigues, Trevisan, Lispector, and Alvim inescapable references for explicit, critical refigurations as well as countercurrents and discursive confrontations in the very sphere of the linguistic-cultural structures that operate in literary communication. But not only there. For these structures act like forces of subjection, hierarchization, and control in social life, in the workplace, and in the everyday in large Brazilian cities. This echoes acutely in the works mentioned above.

Proverbial Formulation as Secondary Chorus

Occasionally in Rodrigues' work, public opinion wears an individualized mask. As the "Man with a Beard" in *Vestido de noiva* (*The Wedding Dress*, 1941, 1943), or as the "Speaker" in *Álbum de família*. His most characteristic and efficient form of exposing the political aspect of literary language, though, operates in a less localized manner, and with a wider reach. It involves a dual game between, on the one hand, the marks of everyday speech, the typification and simulation of trite phrases, and, on the other hand, systemic dislocations and exacerbations. Rodrigues goes about these operations as if conducting a kind of vast secondary chorus. We hear this chorus not just in his plays, but also in his novels, chronicles, and sports writing, where it refigures, in its structural tensions, both the historical matter from which it emerges, and a language that, while shared, "is only common in a conflictive manner."[7]

More identifiable choruses are, of course, often found in Rodrigues' theater. Some of his plays, such as *Anjo negro* (*Black Angel*, 1947), feature more than one chorus. In *Anjo negro*, there is a dominant chorus, constituted by black barefoot women who remain onstage for the extent of the play, opening and concluding it. They comment on "facts, feelings, people"; they whisper prayers, fragments of Our Father and Hail Mary, and they follow a gestural score structured by semicircular movements that either frame or block parts of the stage. Their function is "at times prophetic: the saddest omens are revealed to them" (as we read in the stage directions of the play). While these women lead the play, there is, initially, another group of deindividuated "virgin cousins," condemned to madness and extinction. They intensify and eroticize the figure of Virgínia, the protagonist, while they also antagonize her. And there's another chorus, the chorus of gravediggers, with their torn pants, their straw hats, cigars in their mouths, charged with making punctual interventions, tasked with carrying the dead in caskets and wrapped in sheets.

And yet, if we recall, for example, certain lines spoken by Elias, Ismael's foster brother, white and blind, with whom Virgínia betrays him, we observe in them characteristics of a discursive logic that intrudes beyond more well-defined choral figurations, suggesting a more dispersed generality, proper to the rhetoric of the everyday, to popular thought, to the certainties and the fluctuations of public opinion.

"Only men can hang themselves, women shouldn't ...," "A woman who's had sex – who's had sex that way – should not live," "A dead woman doesn't have children," "You don't rough up a blind man": a series of pseudo-maxims, incomplete reasonings with the appearance of logical deductions, Elias' statements are assertive, but intentionally devoid of any argumentative substance. They are exemplary of the enthymematic logic at the heart of Rodrigues' writing, a logic that is especially at work in those formulations and discursive refigurations of the way in which sayings and premises from the public domain function as substitutes (due to their ample circulation) for possible verifications or deductive reflections.

In Rodrigues' work, *Senhora dos afogados* (*Our Lady of the Drowned*, 1947) is exemplary both of explicit processes of choralization and of the stealthy function of enthymeme in the construction of proverbial formulations (anchored in pseudo-premises of the public domain and incomplete reasonings of all sorts). Like *Anjo negro*, *Senhora dos afogados* also features a triple choral intervention. There is the chorus of neighbors: spectral figures who gossip, eavesdrop, hurl insults, crouch, laugh, and scream, directly participating in the action, marking the boundaries of observation posts, or retreating to the back of the stage. There is also another chorus, a funerary one: the Chorus of Women from the Harbor, which furtively emerges and reemerges, speaking in ritualized prayer, begging in crescendo for mercy and compassion for "the one who died," thus remembering the murder that serves as vanishing point and active curse throughout the entirety of the play. And there's a third chorus, as suggested by the stage directions and as underlined by certain passages of the play – one that maintains a kind of almost invisible but sensibly felt presence onstage. A kind of mute chorus, but a fundamental one: "the sea, prophetic and nearby," always calling on the women of the Drummond family.

In *Senhora dos afogados*, in the midst of those collective figurations and among choral unfoldings tasked with different functions, there is also, like in *Anjo negro*, in the very construction of speech, the insinuation of another expression, collective but attributed to individualized characters, embodied in language itself, and moved by the proverbial mask and by an intentionally incomplete logic. Recall, for instance, some of the statements of generalizing effect in the speech of characters like Misael and Moema: "A woman must only cheat in the conjugal bed," "You can't love a drowned person," "If God blesses us it's because of that, because we're sober," "In the bedroom, no woman must think of any man other than her husband." Beyond the plots and the construction of characters, phrases like these (and like the ones in *Anjo negro* highlighted above) show how language itself and its everyday uses acquire a dramatic dimension in Rodrigues' writings.

diminutives diminutives diminutives

Trevisan's prose also features a similar structural and critical use of "ready-made discourses" – discourses that seem to dispense with argumentation, anchored, mostly, in a reiterative potential for certification, and in an easy and immediate production of affective engagement on the part of the interlocutor. His prose includes proverbial locutions sometimes, somewhat, torn apart, fragments of conversations that are so automatized that they risk being inconclusive. Examples of this include the many one-person dialogues written by the author, where access is given to the speech of only one of the interlocutors, and where either the possible but absent responses of the other interlocutor can be more or less figured out, with no major difficulty, or the muteness of the interlocutor who is possibly listening is simply assumed.

The degree of reiteration in these texts is such that guessing almost always seems possible. This also applies to the many fragmentary references in these texts: from different known brands, to popular songs, to fragments of the Brazilian national anthem (as in *Abismo de rosas*, 1976), and at times to brief auto-references – all of them, for the most part, immediately recognizable.

If a shared repertoire is what allows readers to fill in the missing blanks, in using ready-made language, as Berta Waldman has observed, "the cliché precipitates the creation of a hollow space inside language itself."[8] It stalls possible constructions of meaning and of expressive individualization, and it makes it difficult to ascertain, amidst this reproduction of the same, who speaks in these stories.

The abstraction of the subject who speaks and the continuous recourse to all kinds of expressive clichés are the general rule in Trevisan's prose. They seem to set into action a kind of emptied-out rhetorical apparatus, and at the same time, they make particularly audible a certain consensual use of language, deliberately stereotyped, the excluding hegemonic dimension of which exposes an intolerant society, incapable of living in the presence of difference under any imaginable form.

The hollowing of language points, in this way, not just to an intentional discursive stalling, but also to what collectively constitutes a self-reiteration (at a microscale) of abusive behaviors, something that, in the context of Brazilian culture and politics, relates mostly to a constitutive social project, and a long-term one, unfortunately. Trevisan's work methodically exposes this, in narratives that get shorter and shorter, sometimes just a couple of lines long.

A key and well-known element, in this sense, in Trevisan's fiction is the expansive use of diminutives. Diminutives in his work are sometimes used pseudo-affectionately, but also, simultaneously, in a deliberately unkind form of relegation. They can also perform an explicitly euphemistic function, disguising quiet or more overt forms of violence. At other times, they function as signs of repeated exercises in submission. Diminutives characterize everyday language in Brazil, and they go hand in hand with the sly authoritarianism ingrained in Brazilian everyday life. In Trevisan's work, it is transformed, in fact, into a fundamental, systematic, expressive structure.

His repertoire of diminutives is immense. They include the name of the protagonist of *O vampiro de Curitiba* (1965, included in *The Vampire of Curitiba and Other Stories*, 1972), as well as the nickname of the character-guide of the novel *A polaquinha* (1985). The list includes all the characters in his work whose names end in *-inho* and *-inha*, following the Portuguese-language convention for constructing diminutives: Zezinho, Laurinho, the *viuvinha*, the *casadinha*, Ritinha, the *maridinho*, the *baixinha*, the audacious *velhinho* of the flying trapeze, the sacred *gordinha*, the *mulherinha*, Candinho. Diminutives in his work also serve to highlight various fetishes linked to body parts: small mouth, little finger, small head, small tip, tootsie, little pimple, little tooth. They also include the most banal objects and situations: small coffee, drunky, little table, little coat, tiny vase. All of them are visualized by a kind of reductive rhetorical lens. Diminutives, then, end up echoing inside Trevisan's texts, and they echo from one text to another, and from one book to the next one. They constitute a kind of morpho-prosodic refrain, a choralized affix used to expose the dwarfing brutality contained in those supposed signs of an equally ostensive Brazilian cordialness.

The Mesh of Exteriorities

In *The Hour of the Star*, Clarice Lispector claims – through the book's narrator Rodrigo S. M. – a form of "writing by the ear," writing through listening, an "external," "explicit," and "painfully cold" way of narrating. At the same time, Lispector activates a veritable explosion of ready-made expressions throughout the novel. Among them, there is a series of *-inhos*, diminutives, which are especially noticeable in the story of Macabéa's visit to Madama Carlota, a clairvoyant.

In fact, the pseudo-emphatic use of diminutives ("little giddy," "little dear," "little mirror," "little flower," "little flabby mouth") runs through the whole visit as well as through Madama Carlota's speech as she presents her topsy-turvy visions of a future unfolding for Macabéa. This, in turn, intensifies the cruel way Macabéa loses any perspective of a future, soon after these visions are revealed. The fact that this happens immediately after her visit, having been showered with supposedly affectionate diminutives, only seems to exacerbate the brutality of the accident that falls on Macabéa, as well as its aftermath.

Lispector seems to quietly dramatize here a literary dialogue with Trevisan, contrasting, at the same time, the abstracting rhetorical machine characteristic of Trevisan's work with an intense narratorial presence and a detailed, fictional self-exposure of the writing process. There is a truly strong metalinguistic dimension to the novel, with a step-by-step exposé of everything down to the very characteristics of the rhetorical method that Lispector herself mobilizes.

The device Lispector uses consists in a multiplication of almost-advertisements – "history in technicolor," "this writing sponsored by..." – that complements the series of diminutives. It also includes a succession of popular figures, materials, and brands: plastic matter, scented Vaseline, pink lipstick, Coty (an old beauty company once very popular in Brazil), Coca-Cola, Greta Garbo, Marilyn Monroe, *O Dia* (a newspaper), Rádio Relógio (a radio station that marked the passage of time at the same time it broadcasted news), Lojas Americanas (a retail chain). On top of this, there is also a deliberate insertion of all kinds of canned expressions. Examples include: "May, month of bridal veils, floating like a white cloud," "*de marré, marré*,"

"'Repent in Christ and He will give you happiness,'" "Et tu, Brute?!," "*carioca da gema*," "over there, where the devil lost his boots," and many, many, more.

A kind of mesh of exteriority is thus configured, using trite language. This mesh, in turn, makes Macabéa's inadequacy even more striking. "I too, from one failure to the next," she declares, "have reduced myself to myself."[9] She is powerless against the social grammar of "a city that's entirely against her."[10] The mesh also serves as a background against which potential readers of the story take shape as possessors of some wealth, as people who lead a "comfortable life," proficient in codes and discourses liable to warrant exclusions that affect people just like Macabéa, the protagonist – exactly the kind of exclusion documented in the novel.

"So you, gentlemen, know more than you think and are just pretending not to,"[11] the narrator states, from the outset, registering a lack of compassion in others as well as in his middle-class readership. "Here I'm playing the role of a safety valve for you and from the massacring life of the average middle class."[12] Here, Lispector approximates Nelson Rodrigues in his critical exposé of middle-class imaginaries and of the authoritarian assertiveness that characterizes ready-made discourses.

Lispector's interest in Rodrigues, as her correspondence indicates, predates the writing of *The Hour of the Star*. In a letter to Eliane Gurgel Valente dated August 14, 1951, she wrote: "We went to see a strange play by Nelson Rodrigues, we saw [the actor] Jaime Costa in *Morte de um caixeiro-viajante* [*Death of a Salesman*], he's wonderful, the other ones, less so. We saw a revue at Follie's called *Hoje não, meu bem* [*Not Today, Darling*] ...".[13] The "strange play" by Nelson Rodrigues Lispector mentions here is *Valsa n. 6* (*Waltz No. 6*, 1951).

An interview with Rodrigues by Lispector was published in the *Jornal do Brasil* on January 23, 1971, with the title "O óbvio ululante" ("The Howling Obvious"). The title evokes an expression very dear to Rodrigues in his chronicles, pointing to a kind of tautological, self-evident observation, a commonplace statement without any inventiveness, which adds nothing new: the kind of expression that the playwright used frequently to disqualify hollow reasoning and mere repetition of the commonplace. Around the same time, Lispector wrote a short story "in his style" – as she said at the time. But she changed the title of this story each time it was reissued, until all traces of Rodrigues were erased from the story's name. "Um caso para Nelson Rodrigues" was the original title of the short story as it was published in *Jornal de Brasil* in 1973. It would eventually be titled "Um caso complicado" when it was published in *Onde estivestes de noite* (1974). Soon after that, when it was published in *A via crucis do corpo* (1974), it would take on another title: "Antes da ponte Rio-Niterói."

Although Rodrigues' name was taken out of the title of this story, his influence can be felt all over *The Via Crucis*. As tends to be the case in Rodrigues' work, this book by Lispector includes a synthetic inventory of cliché usages of language, as well as typified figurations. The book also rehearses, in its microplots, deliberately flattened constructions and experiences of objectification. This is complemented by a certain dryness and by a kind of writing that tries to get "right to the point." The result is a narrative dynamic that seems to announce, at a small scale, the method used by Lispector in *The Hour of the Star*. In the novel, however, the critical and calculated use of the most mundane modes of discriminatory expression would gain additional sharpness, if compared to the stories from the 1974 book.

Elliptical oratorio

In the poetry of Francisco Alvim, these forms of critical self-exposure, extremely miniaturized, lead to a form of chorality with tremendously high, sudden, revelatory potential vis-à-vis the Brazilian social field. In an interview published in *Rascunho* in 2012, Alvim underlined the importance Trevisan's work had as he learned to "grapple with ellipsis,"[14] a procedure that is distinctly characteristic of his poetic method. In that same interview, Alvim added other figures to the literary dialogue he described there (including Nelson Rodrigues). Listening to and comprehending particular uses of language in the construction of the socially practical are among the elements Alvim underlines in this interview.

"One thing that fascinates me about [Trevisan] – and in that sense I'm also close to Nelson Rodrigues –," Alvim states, "is the sensibility, the ear for popular language, for the popular and colloquial, which is so rich, so poetic, so full of intensity, of extraordinary veracity. Both of them have that, that genius for language I find admirable." Alvim goes on to cite an example from a chronicle by Rodrigues, where "a young girl answers the phone, her lover is calling, something like that," and, when the conversation starts, the only thing she says is: "You?" "Just that," Alvim underlines. "She picks up the phone and says: 'You?' That 'You?' causes a short circuit in the reader, and it's an extraordinary thing, the force of impact it has."[15]

What Alvim highlights is the force inherent in that use of the "You?," the force that results from dramatizing the links between language and society in the work of Rodrigues and in the work of Trevisan, as well. He also draws our attention to the fact that, with very few elements, and with calculated processes of fictionalization applied to everyday communication, these dramatizations work, in fact, as self-critical grammars. They work as interpreting elements "of social functions and structures."[16]

It's worth remembering that Alvim's *Elefante* (2000) reactivated an adversarial resource that was already present in one of the micro stories included in Trevisan's *234 ministórias* (1997), a book published three years before the publication of Alvim's book. The earlier text is micro story number 110, one of the author's better-known and most analyzed ones. It consists of a conjugal scene where only the voice of the husband is heard: "In bed, the husband says: / – You're fat, yes. But you're clean. / – ... / – You're ugly, right? But you don't cost a thing."[17] Both adversarial belittling constructions oppose, in a self-compensating manner, fatness and cleanliness, ugliness and being free of charge; and they reiterate an aggressive disqualification of the mute woman. This, in turn, sounds extremely familiar to readers who share or coexist with, in some way, that ready-made way of speaking and thinking: the discourse of the "at least it's free," "at least it's clean."

A kind of class common sense is exposed here, a gender common sense, a racial common sense, the reiteration of which, when not problematized, signals the persistence of an excluding social order that uses these pseudo-consensual expressions as ideological anchors. When he takes up this adversarial construction in *Elefante*, and further compacting Trevisan's already very brief text, Francisco Alvim strips the expression

"BUT you're clean" of any major specification of object or of a speaking subject. No story remains here, just an expression, slapdashedly left on the page. Broken into a title (BUT) and a verse line (you're clean), the cut-down version of the expression constitutes the entire poem.

Alvim's poetry embarks on a methodical exploration of exactly that kind of surreptitious politics of Brazilian language, language in its most quotidian usage, at its most imperceptible, as deeply rooted as it is in Brazilian life. It is through these everyday uses of language that prejudices, class divisions, targeted debasements, and silencings are established, fixed. In Alvim's work, as in the work of Trevisan and in Lispector's *The Hour of the Star*, there is no lack of belittling diminutives, which belong to that group of uses of everyday language. And there is also no shortage of ready-made, deliberately half-baked, enthymematic expressions, like in Nelson Rodrigues, presented in their usual, ordinary, linguistic aspect. There is no place for much plot or for rhetorical development in Alvim's methodically brief poems.

It is hardly a coincidence that one of the very short texts included in *Elefante* is titled, ironically, "O gênio da língua" ("The Genius of Language"), the very same expression he used when speaking of Trevisan and Rodrigues in the interview I mentioned earlier. In this text, Alvim highlights in two verses two (coupled) debasing formulas: "corno manso" ("gentle cuckold") and "bobo alegre" ("chipper dunce"). These expressions simultaneously highlight in the poem an imaginary speaker lacking critical insight and his appreciation for slyness and the cult of virile honor, essential aspects of a certain micromechanics of possession, respectability, and command (the kind upheld, in general, by those who believe themselves to be beyond the scope of these qualifiers).

In the context of Alvim's poetry, this is just one example from an active inventory that compiles linguistic markers and different forms of signaling the ways in which relations of social control operate in Brazil. Francisco Alvim activates voices and expressions, fragments of speech that, as Vilma Arêas has noted, "sometimes illuminate embarrassing circumstances from the history of the nation, resisting the passage of time; sometimes they sound pungent, navigating around dramatic lines, sometimes heavy with irony."[18]

This is a poetic method that tends toward audibility. An audibility that makes perceptible – and that intensifies, by its elliptical mode – a selection of grammatical conjunctions that signal the degree of entrenchment, in the country, of an authoritarian culture, anchored in police violence, class privilege, racism, and ready-made discourses of all kinds. Among these grammatical ticks and ready-made phrases, consider those included in the following elliptical poems by Alvim: "FASTING: He spit on the plate he was eating from / They threw away the plate," "THE FORCE OF RIGHT: Things are not like that with me / my right is force," "ARGUMENT: but everyone's doing it," "INHERITANCE: who gave it to him? / he took it / he said it was for him." Property, power, and patronage are exposed and linked in these poems as dominant forces in social relations. Simultaneously, both a minimal syntax and a sharp interpretative dimension of these persistently active historical nexuses are equally intertwined within them.

Interior Disjunctions

Evidently, the counter-ideological dramatization of historical nexuses and class grammars persistently active in Brazilian life is not limited to the work of Rodrigues, Trevisan, Lispector, and Alvim. We only need to remember the experience of deterritorialization (of expressions, behaviors, cultural references, divisions into high and low, moralizing codes) attained in the montage-writings of Valêncio Xavier.[19] We can also recall the undermining of textual models such as the critical revision of the *Bildungsroman* as performed in the satirical poetic cuts of *Crescendo durante a guerra numa província ultramarina*, and of the family-history novel in *O falso mentiroso*, with its sometimes scatological tone (both books are by Silviano Santiago).[20]

It's also worth remembering Sebastião Nunes' *Decálogo da classe média* (1998) and its anatomy of rhetorical molds, professional codes, and "stereotypically typical" mannerisms. The book is a catalogue of types and related figural trajectories that range from the desire to appear "doctor-like," to the urge to "humiliate" those who find themselves in precarious situations, to the mimetic habit of always doing things "exactly like others." As it proceeds to expose, in a pseudo-methodical tone, some standard forms of rhetoric, the book begins to gradually do away with its typological-verbal dimension, which then gets replaced by a succession of figures and by a thick, growing, graphic tangle, set right in the middle of the page, increasingly blocking what appears to be inscribed on it.

It is not enough for self-critical grammars (such as those discussed here) to simply expose standard linguistic formulations, textual models, and commonly applied aesthetic ideologies. Their framing, their mode of presentation, must also be connected to hypotheses of dislocation. As matrixes of transformation, in their critical employment of standard languages and everyday ready-made discourses, they show a need to envisage, simultaneously, both what is being reproduced (in a kind of negative sameness) and the ruptures produced within this framework. This necessarily includes not just standard forms, but also forms of discursive distribution, as well as the expressive limits and the structural exclusions that shape the literary culture to which they belong.

A piece that comes to mind, among others, is the contrastive diptych titled "O Homem-Mulher" by Sérgio Sant'Anna (André's father), published in a book with the same title (2014). Here, Sérgio writes in a way that deliberately takes after both Dalton Trevisan and the João do Rio of "O bebê de tarlatana rosa" (1910), generating another version of this same story. It's an expanded version, not just in the sense that it builds on a predecessor, but in the way that it unfolds, in a discursive field, gender issues posed not only by the protagonist's cross-dressing, but by the carnivalesque figure prosecuted by the protagonist in the turn-of-the-century João do Rio story echoed in the diptych.

In the two versions of Sérgio Sant'Anna's "O Homem-Mulher" that constitute this diptych, the intersections between writing and experience (especially thematized in the second version of the story) are thus tensioned, as are the intersections between autobiography and performance. At the same time, though, the movement between diverse textual models (short story / novel, narrative/ theater) is also tautened – dislocations that are further heightened by the duplication of the story. What we have here are in fact reframings (from within) of these formats, the same kind of reframing that Sant'Anna pursues throughout the course of his trajectory, subjecting the short story to constant processes of conceptual rescaling.

Clarice Lispector, Nelson Rodrigues, Dalton Trevisan, Francisco Alvim (and the Sérgio Sant'Anna of the contrastive diptych titled "O Homem-Mulher"), in their writing processes, mobilize continuous experiences of disengagement, while simultaneously exposing the ready-made discourses that organize and hierarchize not only literary praxis but also social life at large. And it is through these double-scope dislocations (both literary and social) that we can picture with more precision the conditions and contexts in which totalitarian discourses, exclusionary norms, and the conventionalization of prejudice gain social prominence.

These contexts include a significant parcel of Brazilian society in the 2010s and 2020s, a situation shown from a crucially distinctive point of view by Arêas, Stigger, and Sant'Anna, each through their own method, which I will try to analyze synthetically in the following pages. Of particular interest to me are the specific procedures featured in their writing that warrant a critical unfolding between appropriation and reframing.

Vilma Arêas: Framing Exercises

Compared to the rest of her literary production, some exercises in fiction by Vilma Arêas get deliberately closer to exposing linguistic commonplaces. Examples of this are the short stories included in the section titled "Planos paralelos" in *Vento Sul* (2011). Some others – such as "Boquinha" and "Ele," published in *Trouxa frouxa* (2000) – are straightforward registers of patriarchal dynamics. Other texts are focused on automatized processes of racial and social exclusion – historically structural, as we know, in Brazilian society. "Sujos e malvados" and "Algaravia," also included in *Trouxa frouxa*, are exemplary in this sense.

It's hardly a coincidence that "Planos paralelos" opens with a story titled "Lugar-comum." It's a typical tale of sexual advances involving "Mário, the manager," a married man, and a young female worker. It features a restaurant with lake views, a blue Volkswagen Beetle ("the color of her eyes"), wine, chicken, conversations around the office, and a constant back-and-forth between narrative description and very brief dialogue: "Do you like wine? / She said uh-huh"; "I swear, never / Never? / Never"; "Come with me / No."

The dialogue here with Trevisan's fiction (with his banal, erotic scenes and with the quick slippages between speech and narration) is clear and deliberate. It's also evident in "Nem todos os gatos" ("Not Every Cat"), an exposition of police report rhetoric (a "love salad, with murder soaked in crocodile tears"). Echoes of Nelson Rodrigues are also present in this story, in suggestive phrases used in drafts of a news report, and eventually eliminated, such as "Nudity, like death, is democratic," and in the very title of the story, in its implied negation of the popular expression "All Cats Are Gray in the Dark."

Those familiar with Arêas' way of thinking will notice that there is a crucial difference between these two echoes of Rodrigues in her story. The first one, the more or less proverbial phrase regarding nudity and death, strikes a very different tone compared to the author's recurrent remarks regarding class inscriptions and how we display them even when we're completely nude. Class inscriptions are also present in forms of death, in potential access to medical care, in access to prescriptions, and in the life expectancy of different populations. This is even more evident in countries with the scale of social inequalities of the kind that structure social relations in Brazil, where neither death nor nudity can be seen, therefore, as democratic.

The phrase, spoken by a young reporter, is thus shown to be as hollow and rhetorical as other expressions that make it to the final draft of his story. The title, on the other hand, as well as the conclusion – with its vertical layout and its negation of the popular expression about cats in the dark – get much closer to the kind of false-background mimetic redeployment of canned phrases frequently found in the work of Rodrigues. A critical contrast is thus established between, on the one hand, the rhetorical phrasing of the fictional police report and, on the other hand, the negative proverbial axis that guides the storytelling.

Something different takes place in stories like the ones from the series titled "Instantâneos" and in the two stories titled "Na rua," all included in the book *Um beijo por mês* (2018). Stories like these include an examination – so characteristic of the work of Arêas – of dislocation strategies aimed at linguistic commonplaces and pseudo-consensual (but class-oriented) discourses ingrained both in Brazilian linguistic-behavioral expression and in Brazilian life. It's important to remember Arêas' work as an essay writer, with published studies on Lispector and Alvim. Arêas is also a perceptive reader of Trevisan, whose work she credits for its potential to cruelly expose "embarrassing" and "resilient" social connections.

More recent texts by Arêas not only expose these connections; they track them as they take place. This process of registering, as present in *Um beijo por mês*, is marked by the indication and the delimitation of "combat arenas," in her own words. Skirting the usual literary typologies, she classifies this kind of text as a "cutout," thus underlining the repeated gestures of self-contextualization and the self-framing of an observer and a narrator that, purposely, only takes shape situationally. It's important to notice the bullfighting context of confrontation that gives rise, in her fiction, to the expression "combat arenas," and to gestures that re-enact the precise moment the bullfighter finds himself in the same place as the bull, exactly when the bull lowers his head just before charging him.

The fact that the narrator gains a figure situationally is not simply because this narrator speaks in the first person. What's relevant here are the discursive strategies adopted in these cutouts. The choice of pronoun plays a crucial function in the two stories titled "Na rua," for example. Experimenting with the feeling of intimacy that the use of the first-person narrator can produce, this proximity demarcates, simultaneously, the tense class position occupied by both the narrator and the reader. This is a locus that, in both stories, is defined in public space, in conflict situations between the narrator and characters with markedly different living and work conditions, characters marked by evident and radical exclusion, including, in one case, a homeless person.

The first of these stories starts with an "I" and with the narrator characterizing herself as a writer struggling to finish a text. Early Sunday efforts to fend off her writer's block are, unfortunately, interrupted by the sound of a device used to clean the sidewalk outside. The story then immediately moves to a tense confrontation with a woman in uniform responsible for this and for ten other similar cleaning tasks. The working woman is of course unwilling to turn off the equipment necessary to complete her work. The tension that results from this situation is later echoed in the mute irritability that invades the relationships this writer-narrator – this "doutora" – has with her building's doorman. The writer acts, then, as an ironic witness to her own sudden irritability and to some small (but class-revealing) defeats.

The second story also features a brief urban conflict set amidst everyday gestures and behaviors. A quick visit to the bank, involving two separate trips after the writer forgets to bring her bank card with her, sees the writer cross paths twice with the same homeless person. This person twice asks the writer for some spare change; the writer replies with some vague promise to help him out next time, and the homeless man responds with a muted insult ("fucking Paulista bitch"). As she makes her way back home from the bank, the writer hands him some money, and irately responds to the insults he had hurled at her: "I'm neither from São Paulo, nor am I a fucking bitch." The writer then sees fear suddenly rising in the eyes of the homeless person, and she goes from assertiveness to a state of self-questioning: "Am I really a bitch?"

If the harsh, haughty words of the woman in charge of cleaning the sidewalks – the words of the woman who stresses that she woke up at three in the morning and that she still has ten more blocks to clean before lunchtime – give rise to fright and impatience in the narrator of the first story, they also give rise to a series of middle-class perceptions that betray class and classism: "Is it possible that these people are finally walking with their heads held high? Is it possible that this intolerable attitude, as my building manager called it, is an effect of the Lula administration? Maybe she's too young to be properly housebroken? Maybe I look like an idiot?"

This series of questions – which reinforce a perception of hierarchies and social exclusions – seems to run differently to what the second story (which intentionally has the same title) suggests when the narrator is acutely disturbed by her own incisive response, once she notices the fear she inspired in the homeless man. Even here, the approach she takes to resolve her discomfort exposes some ready-made thinking, while also evading structural economic exclusion as the cause behind the homeless man's misery, and transferring to the deprived man the guilt for his own situation. "And what is a man so strong and so handsome doing out of work, carrying around all that junk, panhandling?" she asks.

The procedure adopted by Arêas – laying bare a logic of class, using an unexpected encounter – is intensified by the use of the first-person, which exposes the potentially complicit perspective of readers themselves. This is a mirrored mode of figuration (narrator/reader) of social place itself ("who am I, really?") which points toward an excluding "us." It's a sudden class perception visualized in the middle of a defensive reaction, which emerges as a response to the reactions of people usually deprived of their rights and their voice (the woman cleaning the streets, the doorman, the homeless person).

In both stories, irritability and conflict emerge when the other is apprehended as an intrusion, a bother, a threat – a kind of "violation of the will"[21] of the subject. What comes after that destabilizing unease are automatic, ready-made discourses, as well as the reification of mental habits capable of obliterating the moral sensitivity that insinuates itself amidst the originating conflicts. A contingent perception of alterity imposes itself onto the brief urban conflicts depicted in the stories but, in the horizon of that middle-class I/us that registers these conflicts, no relationship is formed and no alternative perspective takes shape, narratively speaking. It is exactly this limit, this semi-aporia, and the non-unfolding of the (still structural) dispute, that the brief stories by Arêas want to capture.

In the five texts titled "Instantâneos" also included in *Um beijo por mês*, the capturing method is similar, but the discursive procedure differs. It consists in a series of descriptive exercises by means of which recontextualizations and reinterpretations take place. Examples of these reinterpretations include photographs by Luciano Andrade and Filipe Araújo, a cover page for *Carta Capital* magazine, a cartoon by Henrique de Souza Filho (better known as Henfil), and an exhibition by Rochelle Costi. It's a varying procedure, but in these short texts, like in "Na rua," the point is to produce a recognition of the social frameworks that define structural conditions of precarity and violence.

"A black boy, made of flesh and bones, and a white statue made of stone": so begins "Instantâneo (4)."[22] Strictly speaking, this is a literal description of the only photograph included in the book. Three movements follow from the synthesis achieved by this opening: a more detailed description of the visible elements in the photo, a contextualization of these elements (emphasizing the link between art and the world), and the suggestions of a series of hypotheses of fictionalization that invade, here and there, the exercise of observation.

It is hardly a coincidence that "Instantâneo (4)" is the first in the series to appear in the book. It exposes almost didactically the descriptive-analytic reframing method that guides the series in its entirety, and that orients, furthermore, the deliberately propositional or vacillating tone of the perceptive unfoldings in the series. "Although everything can be guessed, nothing can be clearly seen in that faded copy," we read in "Instantâneo (4)."

Arêas' re-reading of a front page of *Carta Capital* focuses on an issue published on August 13, 2014, with the headline "Bode expiatório" ("Scapegoat"). The story on the cover involves a police officer who apprehended a youth on the run, a sort of preface to the discussion on the legal age of criminal responsibility that takes place in the pages of this issue of the magazine. Arêas reinterprets the press coverage, pointing to a vision of violence that contrasts with the juridical asepsis with which the increasing criminalization of the population is naturalized. The final comment of the text is unflinching: "in some cultures, hunger, death, and disease are considered obscene."

A veiled vision of violence is precisely what Arêas' descriptive exercise, as present in these micro-interventions, attempts to dismantle. We see this process at work again in "Instantâneo (1),"[23] which also includes a dialogue – with a newspaper cartoon by Henfil – this one featuring a big man threatening a skinny little boy. We also see it at work in "Instantâneo (3)," where a contrast between violence and impotence is constructed by means of a very detailed description of a photograph of Filipe Araujo published in an article titled "Manhunt: Police Search for Fugitives in Favela Nelson Cruz, next to the State Foundation for the Well-Being of the Child, FEBEM, in Tatuapé" ("Caçada: policial procura foragidos na Favela Nelson Cruz, vizinha ao complex da FEBEM do Tatuapé"). This last text features a movement that inverts the construction of "Instantâneo (4)," the methodological exposition of which began with the briefest of references to the media. In the third of these texts, the conclusive reframing comes after the details of the photo are provided, in the form of an abbreviated list – "the mud, rocks, the left hand of the young boy resting on his stretched-out leg, the boots worn by the police officer."

The last snapshot in *Un beijo por mês*, titled "Desmedida" ("Excessive") is the only one that isn't numbered. Perhaps it functions, overall, as another form of synthesis (synthesis via interposed object, i.e. an exhibition by the artist Rochelle Costi) of the general movement that shapes the writing in this book: to make readers see, to make them realize. This choice of exposition, and the choices made by Costi, are evidently not gratuitous. What we have here is a work structured by the very appropriation of found objects, printed images, urban scenes, towels, dishes, mock-ups, domestic spaces, all subjected to diverse propositions and to investigations that operate by means of stage and photographic reframings.

This may explain why Costi deliberately highlights a certain motto – "a verdade ao fazer perceber" – in the mix of commentary and perceptive exercise (via changes in scale) at work in the artist's exhibition. As I've already noted, this aligns with the usual procedure adopted in Arêas' critical cutouts. It also aligns with a form of writing that, through disagreement, narrative reduction, or commentary, insists, most of all, on redrawing the social nexus as well as the framing device used to structure active fields of observation (which include the observer), from an inside/ outside position that allows one to see, and see again, in order to "get a better view."

Veronica Stigger and Stage Evidence

The descriptive reframings and the narratorial exposure of social position methodically attained by Arêas underline the violent nexus that reinforces both her snapshots and her depiction of conflict situations. Veronica Stigger's fiction, on the other hand, repeatedly shows a deliberate and expansive trail of blood. As Alexande Nodari noted in his book blurb for Stigger's *Sul* (2016), what the writer reveals is the "blood that runs through veins, staining the subject, the atmosphere, and collective history itself."

Generally speaking, Stigger's readers are familiar with the scenes (and the unfolding) that generate these traces of blood. This is what we find in conjugal stories: in the double suicide at the heart of "Curta-metragem," in the progressive agony of "Curta-metragem II," and in the story of a couple trapped in the cabin of a wrecked car in "Tristeza e Isidoro." In all three cases, the situation exposed by the stories is the result of the bloody scenes they narrate.

In a story like "Mancha," on the other hand, published in *Sul*, blood is simply there, splattered in the spaces described in the story, starting with the very first stage directions. It's hard to tell where the blood came from. What we are confronted with is a gruesome after-the-fact scene, the circumstances of which are unknown to us, and they remain so. We can only guess.

The short text here functions as a dramatized and cumulative register of the growing number of traces of blood that give rise to that same story: the blood stains on the door handle; on the carpet; puddled here and there; the trail of blood stains running from the door to the sofa. And the "sonic stain" that functions as the soundtrack for this scene gets louder and louder, thanks to the unremitting noise from an offstage showerhead, the sound of water that won't stop running.

The key elements in the foreground of "Mancha," in its aftermath scene, are two kinds of signals (visual/auditory, blood/water), as well as a (mirrored) pair of women with the same name. One of them, Carol 1, is putting make-up on; the other one, Carol 2, freshly arrived, examines the stains and, in the process, gets increasingly sullied by them.

Possible explanations for the blood are tossed around in the dialogue that takes place between these twin figures: a sofa that broke, a wound, a gush. Lighthearted references to someone who killed a husband and to the bleeding caused by gender reassignment surgery also come up. Most importantly, the same question is asked time and again by the second Carol: "What's that blood stain on the floor?"

No direct response is given. The trajectory of the traces, however, is simultaneously cleft by the trivial living room conversation and by an unequivocal reference to Aeschylus' Agamemnon, signaled by the presence of non-identical twins (the Carols here seem like ironic ghosts of Clytemnestra and Helen), by the purple entryway, and by the echoes of Agamemnon's murder, alone in the bathroom.

This forking is mirrored by the high and low, by the make-up, the trivialities, the tchotchkes, and the echoes of *The Oresteia*, amid the laughter of the twin-characters and the haunting noise of the showerhead. The discordant superimpositions of these elements in the trail-scene of "Mancha" draw out the conflictive writing method used by Stigger. This can be seen not only in the constant theater references, already present in her first book, *O trágico e outras comédias*,[24] but also in the theatricalizing gesture present in so many of her texts. Most of all, what this does is to define a method structured by the conjugation and condensation of brutality and irony in singular, short scenes.

The potential for reverberation is what limits these synthesis-scenes, whether they have, as their basic unit, the couple ("Tristeza e Isidoro," "Curta Metragem," and "Curta Metragem II"), the family ("A festa de casamento"), or larger communities and their Others ("Os anões"). Her strict dramaturgical economy has a direct impact on the cunning definition of a focus, on the exposure of the quiet grammars ingrained in the most quotidian and most structural actions and exclusions of Brazilian social life: racism, vilification of difference, and the violence that spreads over the private and public spheres. Transformed into evidence through the work of fictionalization, these grammars move forward, imposing themselves on us for consideration. In that same movement, the possible, silent, hypocrisy of the reader is denaturalized.

The use of the first-person plural in a story like "Os anões,"[25] for instance, is fundamental in this sense. The text starts by configuring a structural opposition between two groups: "them" (the dwarfs) and "us" (which seems to include the reader in its ranks). From the start we know that the story will unfold with no indulgence, no guilt or empathy, and the reader will be encouraged to follow along, fully aware of this. "Maybe we would feel compassion for them, even sympathy, if their defects of character weren't so obvious."

Difference here rests on a mostly malicious, belittling vision that often operates, like in Trevisan and Alvim, by means of diminutives: "they seemed to have been made on a reduced scale," "little seat," "little guy," "tiny woman," "little couple." Although this may, at first, appear to be not much more than condescending – "they actually made a cute little couple" – these diminutives are quickly linked to a growing violence and to the detailed portrait of a lynching: "the little nose began to bleed," "My husband stomped on the legs of the little man,"

"Aristides' granddaughter ... stomped on the little woman's stomach."

What follows is the merciless lynching of a pair of customers, of two little people, at the hands of families who frequently shopped at a patisserie where the murder takes place. It all happens because of absurd and extraordinarily irrelevant reasons (these reasons, however, are amplified): accusations of jumping the queue, the long time it takes for the pair of little people to decide what to order, the fact that they used the wrong lane at the checkout. The lynching only stops when fatigue sets in, when the need to clean up the establishment arises, and, fundamentally, when the complete annihilation of the two victims is complete, when they are reduced to "an almost shapeless, red mass," to "a kind of mince, blood and flesh, with small fragments of bone interrupting the uniformity of the mixture."

All this is told without any hesitation regarding the baseless violence at the heart of this collective act of justice. On the contrary, there is "complete conviction that those who participated took part in a morally just act."[26] Or better: that those of *us* who participated took part in a morally just act. The "we" here is unequivocal; the reader is methodically included in this collective perspective, in the assumption (the reader's assumption) of an identical, conservative drive to ensure queues are kept in order, and public behavior at a store is kept in check, for the benefit of the everyday life of "normal" (non-little) people. The reader is also implicated in the naturalized conjugation of exclusion, dehumanization, and extermination exposed in this short text by Stigger.

Although the story is narrated from the perspective of zealots, its evocation of a wider class perspective is evident. Conserving an uncompromising social order that responds to defined interests and refusing to recognize diverse forms of alterity seem to weigh heavily in the history of Brazilian society. These actions justify, as is well known, exemplary forms of punishment, performed on anyone who, "intentionally or not, somehow stands against the values and the norms that undergird the way in which social relations are established and recognized, or those who put these values and norms at risk."[27]

Unusual (textual) violence here is underlined precisely by a complete absence of guilt, combined with the defensive indignation of the narrator and the unexpected site where the action takes place (a neighborhood shop), along with the speed with which simple irritability turns into zealous execution. Violence is also underlined, once the lynching is completed, by the furious return to everyday activity and the absolute impunity of those responsible for the heinous act. It all ends, in fact, as if nothing had happened, with the shop attendant removing the mortal remains of the unrecognizable victims, cleaning up the floor with a large squeegee. Once the process of dehumanization and extermination is concluded, the victims are no longer referred to as people – *it* has now become "that filth" that's been pushed to a corner of the store.

This is not the only fictional episode by Stigger where she lays bare extreme collective violence engrained in the most banal everyday situations. But whereas in "Os anões" the action rests on a sudden explosion of physical blows at a *confeitaria*, in a story like "Festa de casamento" she uses a familiar event – a wedding party – to stage, through contrived narrative ambushes, a series of aggressions structured by racism.

In his analysis of Brazil's violent context, José de Souza Martins notes that a growing number of lynchings tend to be related both to "uncertainty in relation to the protection that society can expect to receive from the State" and to "fear in terms of what society is and the place everyone has in it."[28] The family home, neighborhoods, the border lines of the middle class: these are the sites that give rise to collective acts of violence in Stigger's stories. The unstable boundaries of the social place point to violent responses in the face of any indication of change – whether it's the preferential treatment that a differently abled pair of little people receive at a store, or an interracial marriage.

In "Festa de casamento," what the white family portrayed in the story produces is an active, perverse, boobytrapped scenography for an interracial wedding reception held at the grandparents' house. It includes doorknobs laced with pepper, chairs with loose screws, laxatives in the food, adhesive tape in the toilet seats, and invisible nylon threads expertly stretched across the venue, "invisibly obstructing the view." In the first part of the story, a list of demeaning expressions and intrafamilial jokes lays bare a feral and explicit form of racism (shared by everyone, including the groom). This level of racism seems to mortify the fictional narrator, even though discrimination shades the tone of the whole story. Once the ceremony is over, the vile effects of the boobytraps scattered throughout the wedding reception are felt everywhere, causing wounds, all kinds of duress, and the near slitting of someone's throat. The deceased victim of these ambushes is someone from the white family (the groom), which effectively ends the temporary interracial blending of the event, amidst macabre slapstick.

The perverse theatrical character of these ambushes and the chaotic movements triggered by them turn the reception into a synthesis-scene of the brutalities carefully planned out by the white family group. No longer a community of neighbors, or a possible conjugal crime, what this viciousness exposes, in an exemplary fashion, is the family story, and the different ways in which both hate discourses and acts of increasing violence (whenever they are seen as necessary for self-preservation) circulate and are potentialized in this story.

André Sant'Anna, the Monologue, and the "Upstanding Citizen"

If we consider the "fingers down the throat" strategy suggested by Nathalie Quintane in her essays on the middle classes, and if we also consider the configuration of procedures by means of which self-rupturing propositions (internal, deliberate) in the literary field are suggested for vomiting discursive-behavioral conservative pillars, we can see how, as I am attempting to demonstrate here, some tactical uses of the first-person play a fundamental role. This is specially the case when we think of the role the first-person voice plays in potential locutionary games that involve authorial figurations, invented voices and beings, as well as mirrorings, absorptions, and clashes in relation to the reader.

We see, in this sense, how Vilma Arêas operates (in her use and reinterpretation of clippings, and in her incorporation of everyday conflicts) in a way that critically assimilates the reader as accomplice, using a first-person whose tense social place is made evident by potentially conflictive situations. We also see how Veronica Stigger exposes, through fictional familiarization, an excluding "we" that emerges from racial segregation, from lynching, and from active instances of the dehumanization of alterities.

In the writings of André Sant'Anna, in relation to the methodical use of the first-person, the construction, through monologic cutouts, of typified voices with relatively extensive collective reach (voices that tend to share ready-made discourses and fixed ideas characteristic of Brazilian conservatism) is fundamental. Discourses and ideas, in some cases, with extensive historical grounding, and with persistent refigurations and reactivations, especially when historical shifts arise and when potential slippages in the delimitation of classes take place.

A monologic procedure was already present in *Amor* (1998), André Sant'Anna's first book, anchored as it was by a voice that rehashes, all the time, its own anguish. This early use of monologue differs vastly from his later construction, in his more recent writings, of fascist, racist, and prejudiced voices, and from his attendant exposé of the darker side of the conservative mind. In that first book, however, he had already established, from the outset, a structural split that, in his case, and with different components, came hand in hand with the use of monological forms.

In that first book, what we have is a counterposing taking place at two levels. From the graphic point of view, it takes place by means of the tension between text and image, verbal discourse and illustration. At the level of the literary structuring of the monologue, this happens through a conflictive articulation of a verbal flux whose motto is the repetition of "and all that anxiety" (with its intimation of interiority) and an invasion of images and pop references extracted from the audiovisual world (and from the world of advertising and its attendant movement of exteriorization relative to the story).

In *Amor*, a torrential discourse (thrust forward by a continuous self-expansion and by the reiteration of formulaic and imagetic series) is juxtaposed to a movement in the direction of both the anti-subjective and the careful constitution of a dimension of exteriority by means of diverse tactics of objectivation. Among these tactics is the frequent erasure of personal pronouns and of traces of narratorial intervention. An exception in this sense is the reiteration of the formulaic expression "and all that anxiety," which appears throughout the book and guides its rhythmic expansion.

In André Sant'Anna's second book, *Sexo* (1999), this objectivation expands in a story grounded on the repetition of descriptive formulas, all of them echoing ready-made, sexist, racist discourses, religious platitudes, all kinds of prejudices, and deliberately simplistic typologies, such as those used in advertising strategies, in sales and in public opinion campaigns. Hence the descriptive nomenclature by means of which characters are identified: the Executive with Ray-Ban Glasses; the Elevator Operator with a Moustache; the Wife of the Ray Ban Executive, Who Is Over Forty Years Old; The Blonde Sun-Tanned Secretary; the Woman Who Sells Clothing for Young People at the Clothing Store for Young People; the Young Mother of the Drooling Baby; the Kinda Hippie Teenage Couple; and the list of typifications goes on.

The result is a kind of discursive machine that narrates in the third person and that reiterates clichés in a way that organizes the more or less frayed threads of an urban weave of haphazardness, transit places (an elevator, a bus, a car, a shopping mall, a motel), and trivial little everyday behaviors. The fundamental strategy, in this case, is reification. The narrative-machinic perspective imposes the perception of a world moved by reifying relationships and by the instrumentalization of intersubjective contacts. And it configures a story that seems to feed on a calculated form of auto-reification.

In a statement delivered in 2005 at the Fundação Casa de Rui Barbosa, on the subject of his second book, Sant'Anna underlined the intentional use of the "language of prejudice":

> The name of every character is such that, in some way, it suggests prejudice: we have, then, the black guy who stinks, the blonde girl that's dumb, the whole range of prejudices that are usually found in language. The only thing I do is to use that language; I don't write a nice little well-meaning text, I use prejudice in the extreme, to irritate.[29]

The reproduction, ad nauseam and in the rough, of these prejudices creates a completely uncomfortable situation for the reader, who recognizes these prejudices and cannot help but envisage them in objectivized habits of thought and in social practices that also guide everyday behavior. In a novel like *Sexo*, therefore, the story (itself a crude and non-committal autofiguration of objectivized forms of perception and categorization) stalls, at least in the field of fiction, the irreflexive commitment to these habits and practices.

The indefatigable repetition of prejudices not only exposes the level of dominance, in Brazilian society (and beyond, of course), of reifying behaviors, of commonplaces that replace reflection. What is also underlined, fundamentally, is the coercive and excluding potential of that ready-made rhetoric, always on the verge of an explosion of violence, and not only discursive violence. This is made evident in the monologues by ideologically sinister figures that are intensified, in the fiction of Sant'Anna, beginning with the stories published (under the general title *Amizade*) alongside the re-edition of *Sexo* in 2007.

One of these stories, a very well-known one, is titled "A lei."[30] It's split between a detailed account of the narrative procedure used in its construction, and the fictitious voice of a police officer; between author and character; between metalinguistic fold and the exposition of brutal behaviors. In it, alongside the libidinous inventory made by the police officer of different forms of harassment and torture, the text functions as a satirical proto-poetics of the monologues by "homens de bem" ("upstanding citizens") so characteristic of the fiction of Sant'Anna.

"But I don't know about any of that, because I'm fake, I don't exist, I'm only a first-person character, a very strange character who's dumb, a police officer" – so says, at a certain point in the text, the monologic voice of "A lei."[31] Immediately after, and not without irony, the one truly responsible for the text is designated: "the author" – "who is cool," who is completing "style experiments," "free associations," "metalanguage." Or as the police officer goes on to explain: "The thing is that the author of that text ... is me, but it's not me, because I'm a dumb police officer, same as every other dumb police officer."

The rupture between authorial dimension and typified fictional perspective is not, however, simply delineated. "It's me, but it's not me": the same could be said by the many voices in the critical oratorio constructed by Francisco Alvim. There is invariably some crucial interference – the title, the interruptions, the tone – that indicates that what's at hand are dramatic micro-monologues where the voice, though fictionalized, is not to be confused with the voice of the poet or the author. At the same time, the way these micro-monologues are written, cut, edited, prevents the possibility of a credulous, uncritical reception of the viewpoints they present.

In the series of texts by Sant'Anna that are all about "entering the brute mind of the characters" and "finding the language of fascism, of racism, of sexism, of reactionary stuffiness in general,"[32] the split between the authorial procedure and the monologic voice is crucial. This, however, does not exclude the eventual porosity of borders. Recall, toward the end of the story titled "A lei," the police character spreading his own fascism in the direction of a semi-occluded authorial figure: "I am a postmodern first-person, no one owns me, I am metalanguage, the metalinguistic fascism of that fuck of a fascist author who once read somewhere that Glauber Rocha said that when he had Antônio das Mortes shooting people, he did it to purge from himself, from him, from Glauber, the fascist that also inhabited his metalanguage, Glauber's".

The ironic suggestion (ironic because it comes from a fictional cop), meanwhile, makes explicit the anti-fascist political field that gives rise to the monologic fluxes in the work of Sant'Anna. The same applies to the strategy of purging through exasperated mimesis, through a self-vomit or vomit-of-the-self similar to the one prescribed by Nathalie Quintane. The point is to propitiate a self-breaking of the authoritarian commonplaces inherent to some discursive "good consciences." This is done in part by appealing to an ample inventory of catchphrases and, as I've already noted, by emptying these catchphrases, through reiteration.

André Sant'Anna's compilation of "good consciences" includes everything from "the goodness of the Brazilian people" ("doing your part"), to the consumer power of the "new middle class," to the "investments in the Kingdom of God," to the obligation to "privatize everything," to the love of a "fatherland" completely covered in green and yellow (the colors of the Brazilian flag), to the hate directed at human rights and environmental concerns, to finding oneself to be "the best in the world" at everything, living in "the most beautiful country," to playing sometimes an ugly kind of soccer "where what matters is the result, just like in the dictatorship." The updating of these clichés in the enunciative ventriloquism elaborated by Sant'Anna's is ample and continuous.

Sometimes, in writings such as "O Brasil não é ruim," this survey happens from the inside out, beginning with the title ("Brazil Is Not Bad"). Other times, as in "Discurso sobre a metástase,"[33] it can be suddenly guided by an escalation of exclamations: "The market says: Monoculture! Cheap labor! Agricultural Commodities! The Spectacle of Underdevelopment!" These different inventories register, meanwhile (in the heat of the moment, with acuity, and with a sense of urgency), the sedimentation of an authoritarian and regressive imaginary and the growing social violence that took hold of the country over the course of the second decade of the twenty-first century. It's worth remembering, in that sense, that *O Brasil é bom* was published in 2014, before the re-election of Dilma Rouseff, but during a clear expansion of hate speech from the then-rising far right.

It is hardly a coincidence that a certain degree of ambiguity makes itself present when the operation is simultaneously one that registers and dismantles, one that frames and reframes, when it takes place in an inside/outside from which a configuration, a typification, and the critique of them emerge simultaneously. Thus the "meta-spoken fascism" of "A lei," as well as similar processes of rhetorical brutalization and critical displacement present in all the "Histórias do Brasil" of *O Brasil é bom*,[34] or in the section titled "O homem" in "Discurso sobre a metástase," to cite but a few examples.

If what's most frequent, in this group of texts, are anonymous voices, which are marked most of all by their ideological inclination and by the reiteration of certain obsessions, at times they move in the direction of a more or less explicit sense of "we." Such is the case in the violent, group, exclusionary actions thematized in short stories by Veronica Stigger, and in the blossoming of ready-made discourses in the face of unexpected conflict situations in the two texts titled "Na rua" by Vilma Arêas. The collective dimension, whether typified (the taxi driver, the police officer) or possessing a more diffuse middle-class ideology (but with somewhat undefined class contours), is characteristic of André Sant'Anna's texts, but it also points toward a deliberate belittling of any possible sense of "we."

It is evident that this "us" entails some opposites that, even if quietly, seem to function as vanishing points for discourses in the plural. For if similarities point to some collective familiarity, and if these similarities consolidate against various alterities, it must be asked: which alterities are these? In "Nós somos bons,"[35] for instance, the relatively vague attributes of that first person plural ("We're the Good Ones") are presented little by little, but they outline, from the outset, the contours of a certain silent Brazilian majority.

The signals that indicate affinity are evident: "those of us who think that the better times were the times of dictatorship," "those of us who voted for Fernando Collor," "those of us who realized how dangerous Lula was" – the words seem to be verbatim extractions from ultra-right discourses. Throughout the text, however, the explicitness and the intensity of some antagonisms amplify the level of definition of this devious sense of "us": "People who, even with the Brazilian currency at the same exchange rate as the dollar, can't manage to send their disrespectful children to Disney," "half a dozen poor, homeless black people," "it's a tyranny that they so much as try to force us into totalitarian communism," "Black people from the Northeast, poor and with no education." The list signals the groups that are the declared object of aversion for that set of "us." Racism, anti-communism, social discrimination, prejudice against certain regions, and even intraclass distrust are thus underlined, providing them with more assertive, antidemocratic contours, and necessarily politicizing that first-person plural, as well as those who move in the opposite direction and peel away from it.

"What happens when a frame breaks with itself is that a taken-for-granted reality is called into question, exposing the orchestrating designs of the authority who sought to control the frame."[36] This statement by Judith Butler, from *Frames of War*, alludes to the "lives we can apprehend" and "those that we cannot," but it also refers to forms of control and forms of auto- or self-breaking of the norm. It has to do with the necessary re-examination of "received interpretations" as a strategy to demonstrate how these interpretations can break from within, how this can effectively happen.

Similar strategic revisions are found in the literary experiences that I have sought to retrace and examine here, which carry out inventories and critical investigations of deeply rooted discursive-behavioral grammars. I have sought to privilege literary appropriations that, through a gesture of critical reconfiguration, methodically seek to destabilize both historical class positions and middle-class mental horizons, discrediting them and paving the way for a potential, categorical self-purging.

From the perspective of contemporary Brazilian culture, this is fundamental: the dynamic of discursive confrontations that intensifies – as it does in the fictional writings of Arêas, Stigger, and Sant'Anna – both an already strong and conflictive presence of our historical time, and, also, an investigative mirroring conducting processes of self-critical confrontation and reframing inside the literary and artistic fields. And it is by these methodical acts of questioning that their transformative potential acquires a decisive and subtly enlarged political dimension.

6

Choruses Against Counter-Choruses: Parasitic Technopolitics and Geminated Forms of Fabulation

> *"J'essaie de parler de la métaphore, de dire quelque chose de propre ou de littéral à son sujet, de la traiter comme mon sujet mais je suis, par elle, si on peut dire, obligé à parler d'elle more metaphorico, à sa manière à elle."*
>
> (Jacques Derrida, "Le retrait de la métaphore"[1])

If there's one exemplary figuration for Brazil's narrative plot in the late 2010s and early 2020s – particularly during the ultra-right Bolsonaro government – its recurring model ("whether it is an animal, whether it is a whole action"[2]) seems to have emerged from the world of parasites. At some point during the years of Bolsonaro's government, images of the parasite, of the biological relationship between it and its host, were used in several spheres to describe his administration. From social thought (Marcos Nobre) to economics (Márcio Pochmann), to political science (Luiz Eduardo Soares), art (Nuno Ramos), and literature (Silviano Santiago), parasitism gained prominence for understanding the political dynamics in Brazil.

This chapter seeks to examine, synthetically, the comprehensiveness and the connections this parasitic imagery gained in picturing and understanding life in Brazil in recent years. In the face of the "violence, real and symbolic" that Brazilians have lived through since the 2014 presidential campaign and, especially, after the impeachment of Dilma Rousseff (a violence intensified by Bolsonaro's rise to power), "the unspeakable, the impossible to express" "slowly claimed its dues,"[3] as Nuno Ramos emphasized in *Revista Piauí* in 2020.

The analogical–speculative transposition of this amplified perception of violence to the field of parasitology seems to have offered a representational access point to what had seemed, in Nuno's words, almost impossible to express. Thanks to this imagetic link, the density and the reach of the authoritarian mesh entangling both institutions and the management of the nation have become evident. So has the functioning of teleguided, digitally inflated mass choruses, their politico-discursive appropriations, and attendant ideological inversion. These are characteristic expressions of fascist technopolitics.

In a manner that is both contiguous and antagonistic vis-à-vis this parasitism, a series of self-dramatizations – of artistic and literary processes as gemination – materialize: they detail and confront, in the cultural field, the parasitic model. They do this by means of repeated and variable exercises of geminated fabulation, and by the invention (not always particularly strident, but critically effective) of different forms of composition by pairing.

Among these works, my focus here will fall, initially, on the anatomy – in fabular form – of the parasite plot exposed by Silviano Santiago in 2020 in a text titled "Ovos de marimbondo, uma fábula."[4] Next, I'll seek to understand the concerns and rebuffs that bring together and distinguish the artistic processes that give rise to these geminated forms, these concertinaed fabulations, and these counter-choralities, all linked to recent historical experience in Brazil.

We can see, in this sense, different uses of processes of gemination, of non-identical materialities and discursive intertwining. Consider, for instance, the exercises in ventriloquism that guide *O que ela sussurra* (a novel by Noemi Jaffe, 2020), *Lígia* (a video experience by Nuno Ramos, 2017), and *Vaga carne* (a play by Grace Passô). We also have operations of imagetic–polyphonic superposition such as the conjugation of motet, riot, Lima Barreto, and the 2013 protests in *Moteto para Lima Barreto* by André Vallias (2017), as well as Giselle Beiguelman's *Odiolândia* archive (2017–18), and the refiguration of Glauber Rocha's use of superposition and voice-over by Bia Lessa in her 2022 *Cartas ao mundo* (a triptych composed of the films *Asfixia*, *Mercadoria*, and *O comum*, discussed later in this chapter).

In a related line of inquiry, I'll draw attention to some works that also expand their field of production, intensifying, as an active part of the work, the rumor that takes place outside the frame. This rumor is what Ricardo Aleixo's recent poetry makes explicit, and so do many works by Nuno Ramos – from *Cassandra* (2018) and *A gente se vê por aqui* (2018) to *Aos vivos – Dito e feito* (2021) and *Perdido* (2022). This is also what Lenora de Barros accomplishes in simultaneous dialogue with Jasper John's "targets" and with São Paulo's gun clubs (and their encouragement of individual gun ownership), reusing discarded target boards in the exhibit and in the video titled *Alvos* (*Targets*)[5] from 2017 (Figure 4).

Before a more careful consideration of those singular dynamics of composition-in-folding and antagonization via gemination, it's worth returning to certain links between figure and fable that seem to be the ground from which these dynamics emerge. It's also worth revisiting the analytic fields where the image of the parasite gains emphasis, exposure, and elucidating potential, for societies forced into an accelerated predatory and autophagic path. The parasite as critical recurring reference also concerns the means that this society has for understanding itself and for collectively constructing a potential horizon of transformation.

The Parasitic Model and the Extent of Its Reach

Let's not forget that, in 2016, when Rousseff's impeachment was under evaluation in the Brazilian Senate, it was Rousseff herself who suggested, soon after being forced out of the presidency, the applicability to her immediate historical circumstance of the biological analogy between the coup and a parasite. In her assessment of the opening of the impeachment process as the initial framework of a parasitic attack on democratic institutions, the ex-president announced: "This is not simply an image. It perfectly reflects what a 'white coup' is, a parliamentary coup. It's the attack of a parasite. It won't kill democracy today, but if it continues, it will end up killing it."[6]

Employed in various ways and underlining different degrees of reach, brutality, and destruction, the image of the parasite continued to gain a particular hermeneutical quality for the understanding of recent Brazilian history and of its peculiar political conjunctures. It did so from the perspective of a tactical understanding of the totalitarian machine, and from the collective perception of the increasingly fascist manifestations in institutions, in uses of language, and in behaviors, a fascism that became more and more engrained in everyday life. This is a figuration that makes particularly clear the malaise of the present and the misalignment between historical experience and the fabulation of invasive totalitarian anachronisms (insatiable and manifestly indifferent to the agony of the social body that serves as their host).

In 1967, in *Aspects of the New Right-Wing Extremism*, Theodor W. Adorno observed how "it is very often the case that convictions and ideologies take on their demonic, their genuinely destructive character precisely when the objective situation has deprived them of substance."[7] Marcos Nobre, researcher at the Brazilian Center of Analysis and Planning (CEBRAP), in his analysis of the Brazilian context in March 2020, defined Bolsonaro as "basically a political parasite,"[8] pointing not only to his laziness and lack of achievements, but also, in a way, to his anachronistic convictions and actions, a resurfacing of what is "no longer significant" in the present, similar to what Adorno signaled about the so-called new right of the sixties.

In "O virus e o parasita" ("The Virus and the Parasite"), published in *Folha de São Paulo* on March 18, 2020, Marcos Nobre assessed, in the context of the impact of the growing COVID pandemic, the administration that came to power in Brazil in 2019. He defined it as a conjugation of, on the one hand, "incompetence and lack of interest in governing" (public services were functioning *despite* the government in power) and, on the other hand, a "destructive and destroying logic," a strategy of dismantling (deployed from the inside) public policy and "all the institutional frameworks constructed in the struggle against the 1964 dictatorship and in the long work of elaborating and implementing the 1988 Constitution over the course of three decades."[9]

The dismantling strategy comprised, at the same time, a long-term power project, including a prized attempt to construct a new authoritarian regime conceived as the resurrected version of the civil-military dictatorship that governed Brazil from 1964 to 1985. Nobre registered, in that perspective, the strategic aspect of multiple parasitism and its capillarity in both the government and the Bolsonaro project. It included exercising the presidency by means of delegation; renaming hollowed-out programs and projects linked to other administrations; and the deleterious occupation (by military personnel previously released from duty who were also right-wing activists) of strategic organizational structures, which were then reduced to assisting in their own dissolution.

A careful look at the different analytic fields within which (with varying emphasis) the image of the parasite was reactivated in Brazil in the 2020s reveals the frequency, and the elucidating quality, of that biological analogy. It's worth keeping in mind that (to mention just a few examples) this image played a crucial role in, first, Karl Marx's analysis of the State and of the separation of government and social body,[10] and, second, in Rosa Luxemburg's examination of imperialism and the accumulation of capital.[11] It also played a role, toward the end of the nineteenth century and the beginning of the twentieth, in Manoel Bonfim's examination of the links between colonies and metropolises and their effects and historical unfoldings in Brazil and in Latin America.[12] The three cases point to relevant roles played by the parasitic analogy in the social sciences; they help to explain its re-actualization in contemporary times.

After the 2008 financial crisis, analyses like the one put forth by Polish sociologist Zygmunt Bauman in "Panic among the Parasites, or For Whom the Bell Tolls"[13] would return, on a global scale, to parasite imagery, emphasizing once again that "the strength of capitalism lies in the extraordinary cleverness with which it seeks out and discovers new host species" and "in the opportunism and speed, worthy of a virus, with which it adapts to the idiosyncrasies of its new pastures."[14] The contemporary search, in Brazil, for a figure-synthesis capable of functioning as an image and as a fabular summary of an ultra-liberal politico-economic context with an openly fascist nature, would also suggest the repetition of that biological inflection in different disciplinary vocabularies.

Along with Nobres' analysis, we can also recall an article titled "Brasil, vitrine do rentismo parasitário" published by Márcio Pochmann in *Outras Palavras* on November 16, 2021, where he reinforced, from the economic perspective, a similar diagnosis. The point of departure, in that case, was the fact that, with the impoverishment of the nation and the degradation of the world of work, "the life of millions" became "precarious at the same time that the number of billionaires almost doubled." Incapable of "generating new wealth," these fortunes were inflated through the financialization of inherited fortunes and through "frauds and the plundering of the State treasury." This explained the rigging of the state sector, Pochmann noted, which favored dominant groups and diverted public funds toward them by means of "labor reforms and reforms to social welfare programs" as well as "obligatory amendments and expropriation by public servants," among other "modalities of the practice of plundering."[15]

In the sphere of the imaginary and in the realm of cultural practice, relevant commentaries by Nuno Ramos, Luiz Eduardo Soares, and Rodrigo Guimarães Nunes emphasized, respectively and in reference to the rise to power of the Brazilian ultraright, the dominance of (parasitic) modes of acting by means of inversion, mimetic expansion, and trolling.

In an article published in *Folha de São Paulo* on January 21, 2020,[16] Rodrigo Nunes, motivated by Roberto Alvim's removal from his post as secretary of culture in the Bolsonaro government, specifically broached the subject of trolling. Nunes described the usual ultraright tactic (copied from the US "alt-right") that conquers mass engagement using controversial subject matter and aggressive interactions. But he pointed out a key complement to this principle: a certain "lack of distinction between seriousness and playfulness"[17] on the part of Alvim, who lost his post, Nunes concluded, exactly because of the inefficiency in the use of that tactical ambiguity in a too literal personification of Joseph Goebbels. This transformed a provocation by Alvim (with carefully selected text, sets, and costumes) into a paroxysmal exposure of the Nazi substratum of the Brazilian ultraright.

On May 3, 2020, again in *Folha de São Paulo*, Nuno Ramos once again thematized these strategies in "O Baile da Ilha Fiscal" ("The Fiscal Island Dance"). The title of this article, which makes direct reference to a birthday party in honor of the author on the eve of pandemic isolation, also refers to a lavish ball that took place before the fall of the monarchy in Brazil, thus pointing to another ending – the end of the New Republic, terminally ill since 2016.

"The New Republic has a unified patrimony, from Itamar to Dilma, and we're passively allowing it to be raffled off, because no one is claiming it in its totality," Nuno writes, as he goes on to list some of the social achievements completed in the three decades after the civil-military dictatorship: "the SUS [Unified Health System], universal education, the stabilization of currency, the Bolsa Família [a financial aid program for poor families], access to higher education for ethnic minorities, the potentializing of Sistema S [a network of non-profits funded by mandatory employer contributions], the demarcation of indigenous territories."[18]

It is, then, in a mournful manner that Nuno turns to the destructive dimension of the Bolsonaro government and to the identification of aspects that characterize the administration's mode of acting: stridency, a reduced repertoire, and a "potency of dysfunctional aggression" that foreshadows and constantly anticipates the threat of greater fractures in the democratic order. If the discursive machine of the Bolsonaro era continues to head in that direction, "in reverse, down the drain, by burning it all down, by becoming worse and more violent," the mirroring and repetitive character of these regressive acts, on the other hand, suggest a constitutive impotence. "For those in the Bolsonaro administration, it is enough to reverse things, to turn them back," writes Nuno, "they operate through a form of parasitism by inversion, a symmetrical one, with no sense of creation."[19]

Luiz Eduardo Soares, in *Dentro da noite feroz*, a book published in September 2020, also calls attention to that "sterilization by means of (specular) inversion," and to the fact that the sense added to the objects appropriated by the Bolsonaro administration is nothing more than the "inverted image of the original." He directs our attention to that "extremely impoverished strategy," which is offered as a peculiar kind of aesthetic, and the way in which it attempts to restrict and obstruct, by means of a sterile mimetic appropriation, "the space of knowledge, of critical argumentation, and of creation."[20]

As Victor Klemperer observes in *The Language of the Third Reich: A Philologist's Notebook* (1947), in reference to the intentional poverty in the appropriation of the German language in

Nazi jargon and in the uses of language in a totalitarian context, what is essentially at work here is operating changes in the original sense of some expressions, imbuing them with a new meaning, ideologically adapting these expressions, and simplifying everyday language into easily repeated slogans as much as possible (e.g. the adaptation of the Nazi expression found in the Bolsonaro-era motto, "Brazil above everyone and God above all"). In all these operations, an evident disposition to disincentivize thinking is maintained throughout.

In this way, the widest swath of expressions, concepts, and cultural practices is hollowed out and subjected to systemic semantic deviation. This is precisely what happened in Brazil during Bolsonaro's administration, with the debasement of the thematization of slavery (framed as a positive factor by Sérgio Camargo, ex-president of Fundação Palmares, a federally funded public foundation for the promotion of Afro-Brazilian culture); with the discussion on violence against women (rape was reframed, by Bolsonaro himself, almost as if it were a gift, and feminists were portrayed by his followers as "bitches"); with the notion of heroism, linked to the praise of intolerance and the eulogizing of torturers. Furthermore, as it happened in other ultraright movements, the demand for freedom of expression was stripped of the belief system that sustained it, banalizing it as an artifice for authoritarian expansion.

Soares emphasizes that what guided the Bolsonaro regime toward the maximum dissemination of debased mimetic instruments (allowing it to "act like a parasite in order to feed itself") was a structural incapacity to autonomously produce its own projects or contents. This opportunistic appropriation was propagated on a massive scale and, precisely because of its communicational and political force, attempted to establish its own jargon[21] (ideologically lifted from the everyday lexicon). "New words keep turning up, or old ones acquire new specialist meanings, or new combinations are formed which rapidly ossify into stereotypes"[22] – the same could be said, using Victor Klemperer's words, about Brazil in the age of Bolsonaro and of the expansion of its ultraright segments.

The parasitic topic that emerges from the observations mentioned here regarding institutional activity, neoliberal political economy, and discursive strategies from the far-right is not, evidently, the only or the decisive axis of these analyses, which follow their own path of reflection. Nonetheless, it isn't surprising to see the reference to parasitism emerging in the most diverse fields of observation. Among the manifestations of hate compiled by Giselle Beiguelman in *Odiolândia*, there is no lack of references to parasites and vermin. In *A ocupação* (2019) by Julián Fuks, the mask of the host appears from the outset, in the epigraph of the novel, borrowed from Mozambican writer Mia Couto: "I wanted to be conquered, occupied from the head to the feet, to the point of forgetting who I was before the invasion."[23] In a novel like *O que ela sussurra* (2020),[24] by Noemi Jaffe, which contrasts the past ("a pink blanket no longer big enough to cover our bodies") to the memories that contort it (all throughout Nadejda Mandelstam's continuous recollections), the parasitic image also manages, surprisingly, to introduce itself. And, at a certain point, the protagonist unexpectedly speaks about herself and her husband Ossip in the following terms: "branches, almost dead, stuck to parasite roots, you and I."

Opportunism and predatory action are the usual supports of the analogical expansion of parasitic imagery to various fields of knowledge and expressive practices. They generally privilege a figurative typification instead of the minutiae of fabulation, which would necessarily include the cruel unfoldings and the consequences of the parasitic action on the host organism. On the contrary, this kind of examination – from within the biological field – is what happens in "Ovos de marimbondo, uma fábula" by Silviano Santiago, a text published in July 2020 by the *Suplemento Pernambuco*.[25]

Silviano Santiago's short prose exercise is an analogical commentary with figural and fabular dimensions, modeled after some observations by the biologist Jay Gould and after certain scientific curiosities regarding the process of wasp gestation and cruelty in the animal world. Grounded as the text is on reputable scientific sources, it seems, at first, that fictionalization or references beyond parasitology are reduced to a minimum in it. But this pseudo-reduction of scope works, in this case, in the opposite direction: as a kind of thriller, guided by the exposure of reactive behaviors in the host organisms (including attempts to escape) and by the description of the transformations they undergo when they are taken as hosts by opportunistic parasites.

Figure, Fabulation, and Absorption

There is a series of conjunctural analyses and critical interventions that evokes the image of parasitism in the context of Brazil in the 2020s. I've called attention to some of these insights, and it would fall on "Ovos de marimbondo" not only to capture and synthesize, in a literary way, the recurrence of that diagnosis in the social field, but also to make explicit, at the same time, the effects of a certain strategic alignment between, on the one hand, figure and plot and, on the other hand, a possible fabular fold subtly inscribed within it.

What's striking about these commentaries on parasitism is the choice of a biological analogue to describe the Brazilian political plot. That said, the fabular development of this analogy follows, from a disciplinary point of view, an intentionally restricted path. The figure is relational and biological, but the plot that unfolds from it is sociopolitical, economic, or communicational. The physiological threads of the primary plot tend to be put on hold, for they are not in fact the focus of apprehension. The focus, instead, is the parasitic weave, and the way it pulls on the social fabric. The assumption, evidently, is that the reader will have to follow the imaginary threads of this double plot (biological and sociopolitical).

The strategy adopted by Silviano Santiago in his fable is to create an effect of rigorous correspondence between figure and fabulation, intentionally keeping them in the field of natural history – as if the exemplary story were absorbed in its own universe of references (the cruelty of the animal world) and, in a somewhat counter-fabular method, as if it didn't even care about stressing its exemplary nature.

Absorption thus confers on the parasites the function of the Aristotelian "beautiful animal," a model that plot arrangement, as suggested in the *Poetics*, must take as a measure of its own organization, its proportions, its magnitude (size), and its order (structure). The strategy of concordance between image and plot and the self-insertion into the biological scene seem to, in that way, trap "Ovos de marimbondo" in an almost separate tableau among the other analyses linked to parasitism. And while this postpones personal or collective projections on the part of the readers, it intensifies, on the other hand, their engagement with a plot whose unfolding they are allowed to witness from a place somewhat outside the narrative frame.

The contrast between an apparent silence regarding contemporary Brazilian history (a silence belied, ironically, by signaling it is a fable) and the detailed description of a painful physiological process (extracted from Gould's book and from the natural sciences) produces, in that way, a cruel (micro-)*Bildungsroman* that focuses on the interaction of wasps and their host organisms. The exemplary character of the discursive model adopted in Santiago's text (a story told via animals), though it may appear silent, allows it, however, to invade, by indirect means, "art and reality, simultaneously,"[26] even as it sustains a strict correspondence between figure and fabulation.

It's worth noting that, just like "Ovos de marimbondo," Eugène Ionesco's *Rhinoceros*, written in 1959, is also a fable. The diminutive scale of Silviano's characters – insects, larvae – does not in any way compromise their relational attributes or their elucidative scope. Like Ionesco's rhinos, but quieter, they unrelentingly expose totalitarian expansion.

The fable seems to keep readers in and out of mind. It still nods to them, however. It alerts readers that understanding the parasitic plot is something that should interest them: "only human beings are capable of understanding it for their own interest and benefit." On the other hand, the fable underlines the difficulty of arriving at another ending to this story: "In the decade that begins, the future host is trying to imitate the escape plan of the caterpillar from the Hapalia family, even when it knows that both imitation and escape are equally futile."[27] In general, however, a certain distance is maintained between the reader and the tableau-narrative; once the "fatal" aspect of the story is established, a certain indeterminacy is maintained: "there is no ending on a high note, no moral."[28] And if there is no escape, as the story of the Hapalia caterpillar indicates, the clash between "on the one hand, resistance (on the part of the prey) and, on the other hand, efficiency (of the parasite)"[29] persists.

This clash points to both the anatomy lesson by Santiago (extracted from Gould and leaked into his text as an aside, a historical indication – "the decade that begins") and, at the same time, to other geminated structures and fabulations-in-fold, whose critical signs can be traced in the art and literature produced in Brazil after the impeachment and during the years when a far-right group was in charge of the country's administration. And these productions are focal zones in relation to which – amid the fascistic political stridency, and in continuous clash with it – we get a sense of the scale of the experience of the present.

Choralized Reification and Critical Gemination

In the contemporary Brazilian context, the examination of these active experiments in differential coupling, as particular modes of artistic comprehension and configuration, necessarily implies the evaluation not just of the singularity of each one of those methods, of the similarities (or lack thereof) of procedures, but also of the historical situation where this takes place, a situation marked by a certain simultaneity of manifestation. That is to say: while these active superpositions are linked to particular artistic and literary trajectories (which resist fusion and closure), they also respond, in different ways, to the coercive politicization of the present moment, and they construct antagonisms that point toward an aggressive, anti-intellectual context, hostile to any cultural practice with the potential to either trigger reflection or mobilize.

What we have witnessed over the course of the Michel Temer and Bolsonaro administrations is not just a political attempt to restrict the activities and budgets of the fields of culture, research, and patrimony; we have also witnessed degraded appropriations of artistic experience taking place whenever possible. Adding to this, to cite but a few examples, there is also the kitsch ritualization of the practice of performance (as pursued by the far-right activist Sara Winter, for instance), the aggressive ideologization of humor (repackaged as bullying), the dissolution of dialectic uses of language (reduced to the monologic dimension of the religious sermon, or the automatic repetition of refrains, chants, hashtags, and slogans), disputes in the sphere of popular protests (such as the aggressive use of *sertanejo* music – very much liked by agrobusinesses – by groups in stadium boxes in the Sambadrome Marquês de Sapucaí in 2022, which interfered with the Afro-Brazilian music produced by the Rio de Janeiro samba schools for the occasion). These intentionally degraded cultural appropriations stay in the realm of mimesis through inversion or trolling.

When processes of appropriation or reduplication take place as part of experiences of critical gemination (and in contrast to the reactionary appropriations discussed above), the artistic or political reference pulsates; matter and material interfere – they have a voice. They do not dissolve into standardization or formal homogenization. The distinction between the components of this gemination – coupled, but not amalgamated – invites, as we will see, the internal theatricalization of hypotheses of figural and/or fabular superposition.

What critical gemination presents is a kind of poli-fabulation, a coupling (and not a collage) of, on the one hand, defined elements from various sources (previously known) and, on the other hand, materials or atmospheres all produced according to very specific propositions and procedures. This may not sound like much at first, but the (openly exposed) articulation of those elements, of those structures, and of the proposition that is either implicitly or explicitly inscribed in the work certainly distinguishes critically geminated couplings. Recall the playful link constructed by Santiago between an overly exposed biological narrative, and the almost invisible plot of "the decade that begins," rendered in the form of an extremely short and deliberately non-emphatic fable.

In other examples of critical gemination, together with personal documents (a childhood photo of Ricardo Aleixo in the poem "Extraquadro"; some video recordings of the day Bia Lessa's mother died, set between other filmic segments in the *Cartas ao mundo* triptych) and very specific artistic citations that I will call attention to (works by Glauber Rocha, Osip and Nadezhda Mandelstam, Marcel Proust, Lima Barreto, Jasper Johns, Tom Jobim, and Chico Buarque), there is a strong presence of the "prose of the world," as well as a direct, intentional, and often disturbing trace of politics as embodied in the everyday. This takes place in particular modes of articulation: (1) images and sounds superimposed using a computer program, in the case of the polytextual motet composed by Vallias; (2) the use of headphones to listen to free, live television broadcasts, reproduced with minimal lag, in *A gente se vê por aqui (24 horas TV Globo)*, a performance planned by Nuno Ramos; (3) the contrast between pre-recorded filmic material, live performance, and acts of occupation on Avenida Paulista in the exhibition version of Lessa's *Cartas ao mundo*; (4) the brutish montage of violent speech and verbal intolerance of all sorts directed toward Cracolândia (an area in São Paulo characterized by heavy, open drug use, drug trafficking, and homelessness), toward Marielle Franco, and toward unhoused people in Giselle Beiguelman's *Odiolândia*.

These (and other) geminations where nothing amalgamates fully, and which don't create a unified order, don't just differ from appropriations that reduce or degrade references. They also differ from, and stand in opposition to, the obligatory ideological-functional cohesion of certain regressive choralities constructed by apps and social media, which operate, for their part, through a sense of reification, of sameness, and which profit thanks to the unison created by the incentive to follow, tease, and bully by parasitically feeding from and feeding into the neofascist digital machine.

Along those lines, consider that "A Besta" ("The Beast"), the term chosen by the Lega per Salvini Premier ("League for Salvini Premier," a right-wing populist political party in Italy led by Matteo Salvini) to name a real-time device for monitoring digital content and forwarding selected material, is far from random. The tool tracks the publication and sharing of the most popular content, such as slogans and virtual campaigns, the effects of which must be automatic allegiance and mass distribution via digital, parasitic choruses. A similar political machine, equally capable of branching out widely through social media, has been crucial in Brazil for the propagation of anti-democratic content of all kinds, which cements blind allegiance in those who consume it, even when the loss of worker's rights and social welfare advancements is at stake.

In the opposite direction, in calculated experiments in critical gemination, there is no previous medium specificity (there are, instead, differential specificities), no common method of composition, no unification of procedure (there are, instead, very precise, particular, material choices), and there are no choruses in unison (but deliberately dissonant ones). Even when these experiments assume a choral form, this form is layered with different configurations. If there is any convergence, it's because these experiments all work with specific, particular resources – not the resources imposed systematically by the literary–artistic field, but resources that are dictated and configured, on the contrary, by the works themselves, over the course of their proposition and completion. They are also configured by the fact of having – and not just in the book by Ricardo Aleixo mentioned above and discussed at more length below– active, out-of-frame elements that offer themselves to observation and that interact with the other elements that constitute these works.

The intersecting context of growing fascism; a COVID pandemic; the unforgivable death of thousands; a militarization program; the dismantling of institutions; political parties swelled by algorithms, catchphrases, and mediatically spectacularized threats: all this sets parasites and beasts as imagetic-fabular standards. At the same time, it has been possible to formulate figural and fabular counter-standards that self-expose their dynamics of gemination, all the while revealing the context to which they respond, which is sometimes annexed as brute matter in some of the more critically determined literary and artistic practices. Examples of this include the clips of a news broadcast from *Jornal Nacional* used by Nuno Ramos in *Lígia*, discarded targets collected at shooting ranges and subsequently used by Lenora de Barros, and the bullet silently lodged in a body in *Vaga carne* by Grace Passô.

The Targets

On July 30, 2017, a few months before Lenora de Barros' exhibit titled *Pisa na paúra* (*Step on Fear*) opened in Galería Milan in São Paulo in November of that same year, a news report by Renata Mariz, with the headline "Number of Brazilians Taking Up Sport Shooting to Obtain Gun Licenses Grows Exponentially," stated:

> Never has the Brazilian army approved so many licenses for people seeking access to guns. Data from the army requested by O GLOBO shows an unprecedented boom in these licenses beginning in 2016, when 20,575 requests were approved, compared to the 7,215 approved in 2015. With record demand, the expectation is that the number of these requests will only grow. So far, in 2017, 14,024 citizens have already obtained their license, an average of 2,033 monthly approvals, or 66 approvals per day.[30]

The news report offered a frame of comparison using data from the years 2005–17. In that period, according to the report, the number of people in Brazil with gun permits increased 395 percent, from 14,864 people to 73,615 people. The number of gun clubs and gun associations also grew throughout the country, with sport shooting gaining in popularity, a higher number of gun sales, and more gun owners. Shooting clubs made it easier for people to secure gun ownership, even as disarmament policies were being implemented.

In was in that context that Barros began to produce experiences with discarded targets used in shooting ranges and gathered by the artist herself. Around the time of the exhibition, Barros commented on her special interest in "used targets" due to the additional weight of violence that, in her view, is contained in "those decomposing figures," both because of the number of shots that pierce each target during shooting sessions, and given the fact that, in the case of the target-figures, we are dealing with "bodies that never lived" and yet "died a violent death."[31]

Another curious – and key – element in those target-figures determined the choice of material for her experiments: the fact that the mouths of those simplified cardboard figures (hollowed out by multiple shots) function as targets for shooters. This choice aligns with the vast series of mouths and tongues present in the work of Barros, which constitute – as places for the production of language – fundamental imagetic topics in her work. The mouths used in *Pisa na paúra*, focal places for shooters as they aim their shots, underwent a particular sculptural reconfiguration in one of the sections of this exhibit. Crisscrossed by thin threads that act like aerial drawings in the gallery, they evoke Fred Sandback's and Waltércio Caldas' lines, cutting through empty spaces, and they also remind us of police methods typically used to measure and decipher the trajectory of bullets.

Targets are also fundamental elements in a video produced by Barros around the same time and projected at Galeria Milan. In the video, targets work, at first, as prosthetic heads of sorts, covering the face of the artist as she stands in the back of a shooting range, as if she was waiting for her own execution. The target-body then walks in the direction of the camera, revealing, at a certain point, the live figure behind the mask. Immediately after, this same figure is hit with a precise shot to the mouth. At

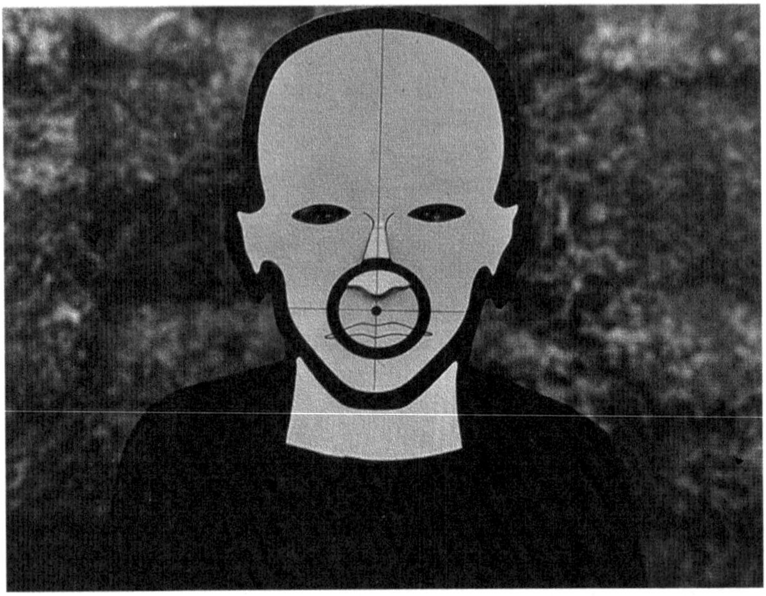

4 Black-and-white still from the video titled *Alvos* (2017) by Lenora de Barros.

that moment, the habitual aspect of the shooting range is recomposed, and several target-heads appear moving on screen, until the target-mask that was just shot takes over the foreground, making visible a surface covered by bullet marks.

The impactful nature of the video is no doubt amplified in a context of violence like the one that characterizes Brazil. It also suggests a close dialogue with the history of modern art, as a kind of re-reading of Jasper Johns' use of targets. Frequently seen as attention baits that highlight the physicality of the pictorial surface, this series of works also exhibit a play between ways of seeing, between proximity and distance, vision and tangibility. What is often forgotten about Johns' targets is the cruelly ironic dimension of their invitation to observers to get closer to the imagery. This is especially the case in works that use paint and plaster figures, the tactile appearance of which seems to reinforce a demand for proximity.

Furthermore, as they stand in front of the target-painting, observers see themselves forcibly thrown into the line of fire, thus actualizing, even if hypothetically, both a situation of "exposure and vulnerability"[32] and the transformation of a point of observation into a dangerous framing. As a living body standing in front of a pictorial target, the observer of the "target-paintings" by Jasper Johns, in that way, becomes themself the main target.

Because Lenora de Barros positions herself in the line of fire, and because she draws her composite target-figure closer to the observer, the video (contrary to what happens in Johns' targets) suddenly places the observer not in the position of the target, but in the equally uncomfortable place of the shooter, the one who executes. Addressing him directly, in a close-up, the video introduces the viewer into the scene, destabilizing his place of observation, and inviting him to witness, in that way (in a kind of imaginary but perceptible counter-field), the scene of execution from the perspective of the shooter. And, in that movement from observer to executor, he is invited to reframe, in the middle of a danger zone, his response to what he sees.

This movement highlights not just the malaise in relation to the place of the observer, or that of the target; it also underlines other vulnerabilities. Endangering the body of the artist (instead of endangering impersonal, two-dimensional targets) points, simultaneously, to other potential victims of real or symbolic violence, of the kind increasingly endangered in recent decades: women (violence against whom has increased immensely in Brazil) as well as cultural workers, another preferred object of cyclical campaigns of hate and defamation by ultra-right or conservative and religious movements.

The Interposed Voice

The abrupt exposure of Barros' face and body, which had been hiding under the target-mask, creates, therefore, a ventriloquizing moment that is responsible, in large part, for the startling effect the video has on the viewer. This is especially the case in the exact moment when the gunshot happens, after the artist reveals herself as an unseen presence hiding behind the target. Like someone waiting to be executed, we see the artist standing right in the crosshairs of the shooter. And we know that there is more than a simple silhouette there. We know who the ventriloquist is; we know who lends her body to the scene and renders the violence of the scene concrete, the violence that subtends the activities in a shooting range, in a sport shooting club, and in the human figuration of targets.

Exercises in ventriloquizing gain different structural configurations in works such as *Vaga carne* by Grace Passô, *Lígia* by Nuno Ramos, *O que ela sussurra* by Noemi Jaffe, among others, but they share some similarities with Barros' *Alvos*. And not just because of the procedure they adopt, but also because they enact some very specific artistic mediations: the non-coincidence of voice and place (evoking Beckett) in Passô's play; the song "Lígia" by Tom Jobim and Chico Buarque in Ramos' work; the story of Osip and Nadezhda Mandelstam in Jaffe's novel. And there is, at the same time, in all of them, a more or less direct irruption of the out-of-frame, the off-field: the stray bullet, hidden in the body, and the interpellations to the audience in *Vaga carne*; the cut that exposes the editing of the most watched news program in the country, in *Lígia*; perseverance in minor key as a strategy of resistance exposed by the fictional Mandelstam in *O que ela sussurra*.

This ventriloquism, meanwhile, differs from the enunciative tension and from the internal divisions of the voice that problematize the diction of so many other works produced during the first decade of the re-democratization of Brazil. During that period, destabilizations of the voice and ventriloquisms – amidst a project of expanding citizenship in the nation (a project articulated in the 1988 Federal Constitution) and the lucrative volatility of the economic markets – seemed to explore, self-critically, the possible place of the intellectual and of artistic production. Both were pressured by antagonizing forces: the financial market and the value of personal promotion for monetary gain, on the one hand, and the strengthening of social responsibility, on the other.

The beginning of the twenty-first century is characterized by the weakening of Brazil's New Republic, by the tearing of the social re-democratization pact, by the hypertrophy of rentist principles, and by (disastrous) military tutelage. In addition, there is a clear restriction of economic resources for cultural activities, as well as a kind of public suppression of some of the most critical intellectual and artistic voices: those endowed with a stronger critical sense regarding not only more direct forms of political action, but also a capacity of resistance in their own fields, in artistic and cultural systems and against a market logic that values immediate visibility rather than the transformative scope of a work or a research project. And in reference to exercises in ventriloquism that emerge from the contemporary context, it is relevant to underline that, beyond being demanding artistic procedures, they also have a tactical aspect and, as Nuno Ramos noted regarding his own works, they point to a "politicization of life that the country has been subjecting itself to, for better or worse."[33]

Three works highlighted here – Ramos' *Lígia*, Passô's *Vaga carne*, Jaffe's *O que ela sussurra* – operate from the perspective of ventriloquism, using different media. Passô's *Vaga carne* grapples with theater and begins with a scene constituted entirely by one voice. "In total darkness, a voice is heard," we hear at the outset of the play, echoing almost ironically the very well-known beginning of Beckett's *Company* (1979): "A voice comes to one in the dark. Imagine."[34] The first ventriloquizing involves, then, a scenic space and an acousmatic voice that is excessive, insurrectionary, and that projects itself voraciously toward all kinds of matters:

> Once in a while, when you notice that the glass cracked for no apparent reason. Or even the frog that jumped, one day, to an unusual height. Or when the faucet dripped. Endlessly, endlessly, endlessly, endlessly ... Go see what's wrong with it! It's hard to know, but it's possible that this is not a physical event that has to do with matter, but, yes, it's matter itself, invaded by voices.[35]

This instance of (explicit) ventriloquizing comes hand in hand with another one: a deliberate ventriloquizing of a principle of composition that not only takes after Beckett, but that became fundamental for dramaturgy and for contemporary literatures. What I have in mind is the recurrent use of an independent performative voice and of essential alterities between voice and bodies, between source and locution. For Passô seems to stage, simultaneously, an untimely fluctuation of the voice by different matters, a conflictive coupling (exposed by gestures) between voice and body, and an investigative meta-scheme regarding the procedures that refigure and guide the play.

Once these elements are exposed (the act of autonomizing; the performative character of the voice; the non-coincidence of physical action and discourse), *Vaga carne* chooses, as a temporary landing, a feminine body that seems to be "inert," "with no action in the world."[36] Occupying the body of this woman, the same voice goes on to describe it in detail, from the inside, weaving together hypotheses about this body and questions regarding its previous existence: "I don't even know what the body of this woman looks like from the outside any more. Who is she? What does she do? Why is she here, now? Her back looks exhausted; can you see that from there? Does she smoke? Was she always a woman? What color is she?" And the voice continues to lend movement to the woman, moving a finger, balancing parts of her body, opening and closing her eyes, occupying the body of this woman with loud words coming from the place where the audience is: "We are going to occupy the body of this woman with words! This woman here is only a microphone, poor thing, she has nothing to say! Yell out words, all of you, I'll put them here, inside her!"

Let's not forget that the definitive version of *Vaga carne* premiered in 2016. Its first reading was in 2013, in the context of the project titled "Janela de dramaturgia" in Belo Horizonte, just as the Jornadas de Junho were taking place. It's hard not to link these events. It's hard to ignore the echoes of these events in that voice that oscillates from one matter to another, in that speech that remains continuously in flux, that interpellates restlessly. It's an echo of other voices, many other ones, voices that occupied the streets. There is also, furthermore, in a relentlessly dramaturgic manner, something of a feverish demand, an urgency, a trace of the indeterminacy that characterized those days of intense street demonstrations.

In that specific context, Passô gave an interview and made some direct remarks regarding the link between theater and insurrection. These are her observations, dated June 21, 2013:

> I think that – and you can even draw a parallel with everything that has happened in Brazil – we are living through an insurrection, an indescribable human mobilization. What is taking place today, with all these protests, is a country trying to name very urgent feelings coming from the population. That's what works of art do, as well. They don't necessarily name anything, but they try to create forms for those feelings. For that urgent need.[37]

Intermittent material engagements and successive interlocutions keep the voice in continuous motto mode. Even inside the female body that contains it, the voice discovers a gestating fetus, an orthopedic surgical pin. It finds a bullet that was never extracted. Once the bullet is found in the body, a decisive excursion to the off-field of the text is completed, projecting into this black female body a violent urban-everyday, an everyday of stray bullets and preferential target-bodies. This is a scene of violence that expanded during the 2013 protests, truculently and with a disproportional use of force on the part of the military police. And even though the reference to the inactive bullet, absorbed by the body, does not yield any further major outcomes in the play, the discovery of the bullet comes hand in hand, nonetheless, with a kind of narrative acceleration.

The more direct interactions with the public, the self-inflicted incision on the body, the verbal hollowness and verbal lapses that keep getting longer and longer: all of this ends up eventually interrupting the verbal flux of the play. It thus reduces it to an acoustic atmosphere, to the space of the scene, and to a growing awareness of the performer's body – "woman," "Black woman," "here." This presence gains increasing definition and place. "Now I know who she is! I know! She is a woman, she is Black ... Wait! Now I know! She is here, today, in front of you, and she would like to say that ..."[38] A consciously split (but coupled) figuration of body and voice is maintained. Hence the repeated non-coincidence of pronouns (I/she).

Lígia,[39] by Nuno Ramos, is a video publicly shown for the first time on August 31, 2017, on the website www.aarea.com, a year after the impeachment proceedings against Dilma Rousseff began. In it, duplication and disagreement are also superimposed. The conjugation between a process of coupling (of a 1974 song by Tom Jobim and Chico Buarque, revisiting bossa nova, and the image as well as the voice of the anchors of *Jornal Nacional* in 2016) and a methodic misalignment (between sound and image, between two different time frames, between two referents) is the organizing principle of this work.

In this case, the initial material consists of broadcastings of *Jornal Nacional* aired on March 16 and August 31, 2016; the first date corresponds to the day when conversations between Rousseff and Lula (on the possibility of him becoming her chief of staff) were leaked; the second date marks the day when the Senate approved impeachment proceedings against Rousseff. Regarding the first date, there is a note made by Ramos in the heat of the moment, titled "JN, 16.3.2016," and later disseminated by the artist himself, which explains dramaturgically the choices behind that broadcast in particular, beyond the historical significance of the leaked conversations between Rousseff and Lula:

> When Moro made public the recorded conversations between Lula and Dilma, along with many other recordings, *Jornal Nacional* transformed into a feast; the recordings were a godsend. Its anchors read the transcriptions they had just received (recordings from the conversations between the two politicians were made available that same afternoon) live, like warm little bread rolls coming straight out of the oven, evincing careless informality (given the hastiness of the journalistic review) with the materials they were reporting on, so freshly arrived that they would read them from printouts instead of using teleprompters ... They did not realize that, as the transmission went on, they stopped acting as journalists and became actual actors, in a memorable (Freudian) slip.[40]

What makes this journalistic moment a slip also points to the method adopted in *Lígia*: "Transposing the boundary between narrating and acting, they [the news anchors] no longer read – they interpreted, they intoned, they even performed a certain kind of facial miming, without any of the distance, the true or false distance, that they usually display as part of their reporting."[41] The re-reading of the news broadcast from March 16 in Nuno's video would accentuate, through clips, some of the gestures made by the anchors that signaled the extent of their performance: "Difficulties with timing, small issues with the audio, the activation of the wrong camera accentuated this. The anchors and producers had lost the steadfastness of their tribune, and their studio, that silver fishbowl, seemed to transform into an integral part of the action that the news pretended to narrate from a certain distance."[42]

The unintentional exposure of the undeniable activism of journalists defending and instigating the impeachment would suggest, then, the appropriation by the artist of this audiovisual material. In addition to the news televised on the day the conversation between Dilma and Lula was made public, *Lígia*'s video material also includes recordings from the day the impeachment was approved, when the country's right-wing forces achieved a desired political reorientation (which they could not obtain electorally) and a fascist-like coup-shift in the country's leadership.

The video editing work, involving images and sound from TV Globo news broadcasts, is more evident, perhaps, in its acoustic layer, which cuts out some syllables in the speech of anchors William Bonner and Renata Vasconcellos and reuses this speech to reconstitute the song "Lígia," which then replaces the text read out by the anchors, though still in the voice of both journalists. Superimposing the song onto the text of the newscast, in an intermittent kind of way (by the edited audio and voices), evokes, rhythmically, the syncopated beat of bossa nova. It also, on the other hand, draws attention to the mismatch between the happy dream of modernization corresponding to the original period of bossa nova (already an object of belated lament at the time the song "Lígia" was composed) and the aggressive exposure – via televised news broadcasts – of the destruction of a social pact and of the three decades of democratic interregnum in Brazil.

A different kind of *Jornal Nacional* was broadcast, then, every day, for a month, at Aarea.com, in the time slot corresponding to the real *Jornal Nacional* (Monday to Saturday, around 8:00 p.m.). It even included cuts for commercial breaks. In Nuno's version, the news anchors sing Tom Jobim and Chico Buarque and point toward certain possible story finales to come – the end of the New Republic; of inclusive policies; of respect for the ballot box; of a time that, in fact, seemed to have no place for bossa nova or for any of its everyday infra-epiphanies. Repeated daily, the exposure of the show's unequivocal ideological commitment was amplified through its redefinition of content, as was the pseudo-theatricality of the news presenters. Sung by the generally hypertrophied voice of TV Globo, "Lígia" would move, in Ramos' work, from personal melancholy to civic grief, thus rising to the status of a collective funeral song, as well as gaining a strong sense of dissent amidst the untruthful media and the parliamentary consensus regarding both the deposition of the elected president and the reduction of painfully attained rights.

When the novel *O que ela sussurra* was published by Noemi Jaffe in 2020, the political appropriation of the country by right-wing groups was strengthened by the election of Jair Bolsonaro, by the expansion of military tutelage, and by the growing instability of democratic institutions. A double ventriloquizing dialogues with that situation in Jaffe's novel. First, there is Nadejda Mandelstam lending her voice to poems by her husband over the course of 25 years, before the publication of those poems was authorized in the Soviet Union. Second, there is the fictionalization of this unfolded diction, the mode of expression becoming a motto, and transforming itself into the narrative method for Jaffe's historical novel.

"A quiet subversion, which in some way escapes the regime's control, like those planes that, flying so low and so fast, manage to evade even the most powerful radars":[43] the tactical whisper as a form of preserving and disseminating Osip Mandelstam's works. Repetition, even the repetition of simple formulations, represents, in the novel, an exercise in resistance. This is evident in the partially invented episode of the bus, where a woman, after bumping into Nadejda and apologizing, says: "We're strong, like the devil." Soon after that, everyone else started repeating the same phrase, "like a harmless but resilient chorus that could carry an empire, stop an army, implode a regime with that phrase."[44]

This is what Nadejda's memorizing of Osip Mandelstam's poems suggests for Jaffe: the force of almost imperceptible gestures of resistance; the voice that offers itself as host for someone else's voice, for the text of an Other, forging, for herself, a sideways narratorial perspective, like a figure interposed in its own story. However, when the fictionalized voice is that of the poet Anna Akhmátova, what it talks about is Nadejda. Thus, the guiding procedure of the narrative is repeated, but this time, the life of the Other who is ventriloquized is the life of the one who usually lends her voice to another.

What distinguishes the first segment of the novel is repeated, but with a different addressee: first, in the monologue, Nadejda addresses her husband (intercut with fragments of Mandelstam's poems); then, toward the end, the other monologue is addressed to Nadejda by a fictional Akhmátova (who performs, at a certain point, a narrative function in the novel). This modifies, in part, the general focus of the novel, which concludes in a kind of semi-epistolary way: "Outlive us, Nadjenka, Nadjucha, be the pain of a hoarse laugh, because we, so much less than stones, only have enough strength to die."[45]

In *Vaga carne*, a nameless voice, nonstop, insurrectionary, in search of configuration, keeps itself in a split field even after a brief scene where it recognizes the body (female, Black) it inhabits. In Ramos' *Lígia*, the interspersed voice is the voice of the remixed newscast, exposing the media's authoritarian activism. It is also the voice of the song by Tom Jobim and Chico Buarque, mourning – intermittingly – not just a difficult kind of love, but the very impossibility of bossa nova outside its own creative context and in those two necessarily gloomy settings (the dictatorship, in 1974 when the song was launched, and post-impeachment Brazil, when Nuno Ramos' video was edited). What is framed here, in the video, is the ironical vocal crossover of a national TV program and the very intimate dimension of the *samba-canção*, refiguring, in a dissenting manner, the mourning chant.

Hate Choruses

If ventriloquism as a method of artistic gemination deliberately unfolds (and internally exposes) the conflict already present in some processes of enunciation, other similar methods entail (through superposition and montage) more expansive forms of choralization. In the case of the tripartite project that Giselle Beiguelman titled *Odiolândia*, for instance, three vast archive-speeches are constituted through a compilation of comments published on social media regarding, first, the occupation of Cracolândia by the military police between May 21 and June 9, 2017; second, the execution of Marielle Franco, city councilor in the Municipal Chamber of Rio de Janeiro, on March 14, 2018; and third, the fire at, and subsequent collapse of, the Wilton Paes de Almeida building at Largo do Paissandu, in São Paulo (an abandoned building that had been occupied since 2003 by a group of people associated with housing movements), on May 1, 2018.

These three dates, expressive of the growing virulence of the police, of political violence, and of the increasingly fascist dimension of public opinion (and predating the 2018 Brazilian elections), also point to the enormous support base constructed digitally by the ultra-right, a massive base that tends to be intensely activated in events with significant public repercussions, like the ones selected by Beiguelman. Like some of her other works, many of them guided by artistic-conceptual archival practices, these compilations underwent more than one formatting process.

The first part of *Odiolândia* was originally presented as a video installation for *São Paulo não é uma cidade: as invenções do centro*, an exhibition that took place at SESC São Paulo on May 24, 2017. The video[46] was included in other exhibitions, and its main feature is the fact that it does not show any images other than the visual reproduction of some comments that circulated on the internet, regarding police actions at Cracolândia. The comments are shown sequentially and horizontally on a dark screen, while real audio (from the military police, from shots, helicopters, the voices of squatters, the voices of the policemen, from dog barks, screams, and bursts of gunfire) can be heard on the video's audio track.

The second part of the project, thematizing the assassination of Marielle Franco and Anderson Gomes in downtown Rio de Janeiro, was read in a performance at the Museu de Arte do Rio (MAR) in December 2018. And the third part, with samples of hate speech against housing movements[47] (hate speech spouted on the occasion of the collapse of the Wilton Paes de Almeida building), was partially read on Rádio USP (the University of São Paulo radio station) by the artist, and it was also published at that time on her website.

At the end of 2018, all three segments were published in booklet form by N-1 Edições, allowing for three long choral forms of speech to take shape there, forms of multiple speech composed of phrases[48] taken from protests, all of them driven by hate; by violent rejection of all kinds of alterity; by regional, social, and racial prejudice; by xenophobia; by homophobia; by misogyny. Simultaneously, these forms of speech came intertwined with an unabashed defense of militarization, executions, exterminations, and agendas such as the decriminalization of gun ownership, the institution of the death penalty, and the abolishment of age limits for criminal responsibility. Hence the title of the book (*Odiôlandia, Hateland*). As Beiguelman writes, "The title of this work emerged from the content of publicly posted messages. The vast majority of these messages favored a law enforcement approach to [Cracolândia] and they favored using guns against drug users; they also expressed the desire to see these same policies applied to other groups. *Nordestinos*, landless people, and gays were some of the targets highlighted."[49]

In the montage of each choral segment, Beiguelman seems to evoke the "cidadãos de bem" ("upstanding citizens") speeches of André Sant'Anna. She also seems to incorporate procedures characteristic of the "theatricalization of the real," as well as some brutish appropriations of documentary material (such as those by the poet Kenneth Goldsmith, creator of Ubu Web). Beiguelman's procedure is not only to some extent similar to what takes place in *Abril*[50] (2016) by Gabriela Carneiro da Cunha and Eryk Rocha (a play performed by Carolina Virguez and staged at the Castelinho do Flamengo, in Rio de Janeiro). It is also comparable to what we find in the book *Sessão*, published by Editora Luna Parque in 2017 and featuring poems constructed from fragments of speech from the final congressional vote in Rousseff's impeachment process.

In sync with those appropriations ("dissociated from names and images"[51]), Beiguelman's tripartite *cordel* (booklet) comprises an archive-work that she herself refers to as the "serpent's egg," to the extent that it constitutes a significant repository of the topics and the rhetoric of intolerance and authoritarianism in Brazil during 2017 and 2018. The sequential montage of the three textual fluxes (with a brief interval between each), and the evidence of the rhetorical interrelationship between them, underlines the evolving maturity of that "egg." In contrast, however, with this triple partition, there is also, simultaneously, a strong parallel between the fluxes. The three variants present a similar mode of fabulation through parasitic self-reproduction, and an inertial reduplication of contents that encompasses an almost inevitable (but involuntary) self-figuration of these hate choruses as a kind of monologue-in-several-homogenized-voices.

Montage, Motet, Melee

The choral method elaborated by André Vallias in *Moteto para Lima Barreto*[52] is of a different order. Vallia's poem is a polyphonic palimpsest in which two time frames – the beginning of the Brazilian Republic and the agony of the "New Republic" – converge and become interrelated. The voices of Numa Ciro, Paulo Sabino, and Vallias alternate in the poem, and three sets of materials are superimposed in it.

We have, on the one hand, the verbivocovisual invocations of a series of names: some of the pseudonyms used by Lima Barreto (Jonathan, Xim, Horácio Acácio, Inácio Costa, Pingente, Barão de Sumaret, Eran, Amil, J. Caminha, S. Holmes, Phileas Fogg, Ingênuo, Tradittore) – some of them already known, others doubtful, others uncovered recently by Felipe Botelho Corrêa, a researcher who compiled, in 2016, a series of unpublished writings by the author.[53] Corrêa emphasizes that, although pseudonyms were a common practice at the time, these fictitious names proved particularly valuable in "satirical texts with social or political commentary."[54]

Another set of materials is a series of selected fragments from Lima's chronicles, published between 1917 and 1918, in which the impact of the 1917 Russian Revolution is evident. Lima concluded one of them, from May 2018, with the following statement: "The face of the world has changed. Ave Russia!" The quotes are from "Vera Zasulitch," published by the magazine *Brás cubas* on July 14, 1918; "São Paulo e os estrangeiros," published in *O debate* on October 6, 1917; and "No ajuste de contas ...," published on May 11, 1918, in the newspaper *A.B.C.*

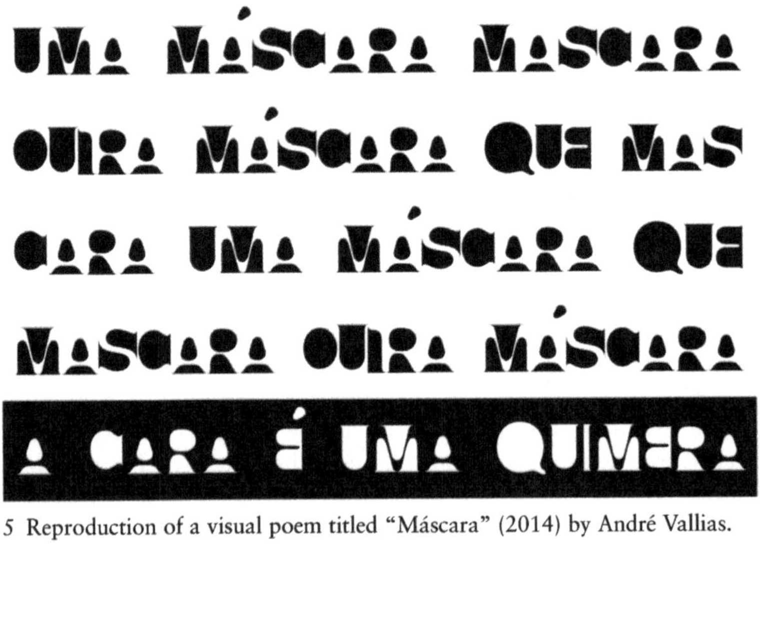

5 Reproduction of a visual poem titled "Máscara" (2014) by André Vallias.

The excerpts included in Vallia's work are historical commentary that, while embedded in the Brazil of the Old Republic and of the first uprisings and workers' strikes, also illuminate the nationwide mass mobilizations of June 2013, the context of the 2016 coup, and the subsequent election of a candidate from the ultra-right.

Vallia's poem vocalizes some of these fragments. The poem incorporates Lima's comments on the Proclamation of the Republic: "the patrols walked the streets, armed with rifles," "the city's physiognomy was one of stupor and fear," "it gradually accentuates the features it already had at birth." It also incorporates Lima's views on plutocracy and its "continuous, constant influence, day and night, on the law and on the ruling classes, in favor of their insatiable enrichment," draining "all the sweat and blood of the country into their vaults, in the form of high prices and high interest rates." It also includes his observations about hypocritical religious groups, the legal system, and the way these institutions serve the oligarchies: "the wealthy of Brazil have never pretended to be more religious than now,"[55] "a social reform must be instigated against 'the Law' they preach, as their god is already dead."[56]

Lima Barreto's observations intertwine the two time frames of the motet (the beginning of the Republic and the protests of June 2013), in a way that makes them mutually project each other. The poet adds a third component to the motet, to the fragmented reading of the excerpts and the invocation of Lima's fictitious names (a list that makes him a legion). This third component is a group of poems contemporary with or directly linked to the 2013 Jornadas – six visual poems in total: "Poema civil n-1," "Modernidade," "Simetria," "Máscara" (Figure 5), "Madeira de lei" (Figure 6), and "Opróbrio."

In these poems, refigurations of topics similar to those in Barreto's chronicles resurface in a different context: the State control by "bankers" (the "Ex-tate," "everything is under control"); police brutality against poor people, Blacks, and insurgents ("que a lei de madeira dura / mais que a madeira de lei"); the conjugation of two "Belo Montes" (the rural community in Canudos, Bahia, and the hydroelectric plant in the Xingu River in the state of Pará); the imprisonment of Rafael Braga (a homeless man accused of carrying two plastic bottles of detergent during the June 2013 protests); and the characteristic

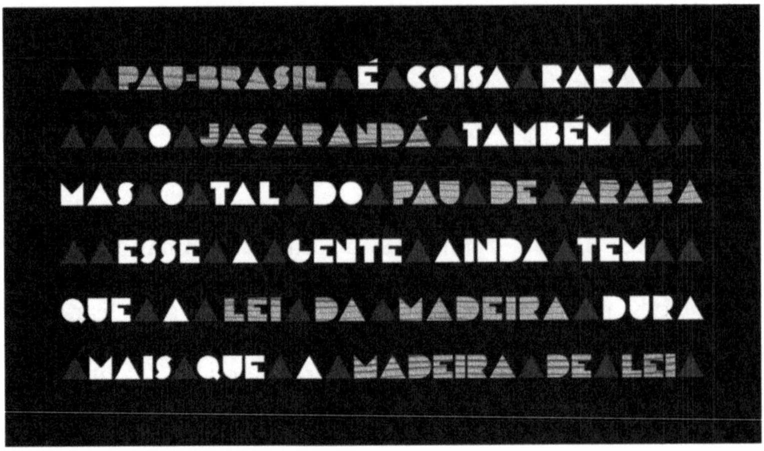

6 "Madeira de lei" (2013), a visual poem by André Vallias.

selectivity of judicial processes in Brazil ("opprobrium / the poor Black man / imprisoned / a scapegoat") (Figure 7), echoing the fear, the rifles, the "jackals and hyenas in the service of the bourgeoisie" described by Lima Barreto.

All those refigurations operate, from the perspective of a historical semantics, as almost-rhymes that intensify the links indicated by that double fabulation. And they also allow a heterochronic projection of Barreto's diagnosis, which is almost whispered in the motet: "the time is now for radical measures". The coupling of two time frames works as the fundamental element in this composition-by-gemination of the poem, but its choralization process goes well beyond the echoic fabular duplication. Hence the list of Lima Barretos (the list produced with his pseudonyms) behind different masks. Hence the increasing density of the acoustic dimension, beyond the three guiding voices (Numa Ciro, Paulo Sabino, and Vallias), including a composition by Marlos Nobre and other extremely brief insertions. And there is also the concern (proper to the motet) with the increasing complexity of the verbal plot – the spoken word and the printed word, the visible and the audible, verbal materials in a situation of overlap, on a spiral path, or in poster mode.

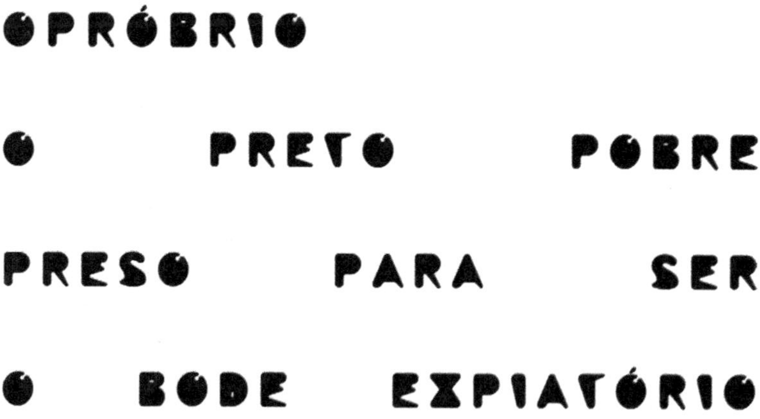

7 Reproduction of a visual poem titled "Opróbrio" (2013) by André Vallias.

The "Motet for Lima Barreto" – constructed electronically – presents itself at one and the same time as an active chorality and as a self-exposing configuration (in echo and in differentiation) with components that define and also segment it in a dual timeline. And, as part of a continued investigation of the poem as an open, interrelational, and intermedial structure – and of its own epic-critical dimension (different from other poems by Vallias such as *Oratório* and *Totem*) – the motet performs a function of differentiation not only within the poet's method but also within the experiments in geminated structures and choral forms that I am considering in this chapter.

Voice-Over and Choralization

Although the author focuses on the same urban area that gave rise to the first segment of Beiguelman's *Odiolândia* (Largo do Paissandu, in the center of São Paulo), Bia Lessa's *Cartas ao mundo* works with other choralization processes. Lessa's project began as an occupation, eventually resulting in a triptych of distinct and autonomous films: *Asfixia*, *Mercadoria*, and *O comum*.[57] A series of recurring images and references run through all three films, as does a tension between dystopia and utopia. The titles of these films signal the different issues broached by *Cartas ao mundo*, the documentary-manifesto that took shape in these films and that eventually spawned, in 2022, performances and exhibitions at SESC on Avenida Paulista.

Cartas ao mundo evolved during the years 2020–1, as a response to the COVID pandemic and the impossibility of regular, in-person interventions in buildings and public spaces in Largo do Paissandu as originally conceived by Lessa. The configuration of this project geminated a real place and a digital place; Lessa opted for a virtual occupation of real, abandoned or underused spaces in the region, using exhibitions, projections, and installations that took place within the films, in a digital realm. This choice was accompanied by another one: the experience of an intermittent voice-over, throughout the entire film triptych, performed with her own voice.

This was done in intentional dialogue, as I already noted, with the voice-over used by Glauber Rocha in films such as *Claro* (1975) and *Di* (1977), or in his series of excerpts from the TV program *Abertura* (1979). The exposure of the authorial voice, in the case of Bia Lessa, makes it an additional active component amid the vast process of compilation and montage at the heart of her triptych, a process elaborated, at a certain point, as a refiguration-in-simultaneity of the tripartite structure of Dante's *Divine Comedy* (but without any kind of ascending or infernal progression).

Lessa's voice appears at the outset of all three films. But instead of overusing her voice, she includes it as one more acoustic element in the triptych, and what starts as a restricted focus on the sound of her voice soon takes on a choral dimension. Fragments from several films by Rocha and extracts from interviews with, and interventions by, the filmmaker enter into Lessa's triptych. Words spoken by other artists and intellectuals also come in, as do bits of lectures, poems, conversations, artists' writings, and all kinds of speech fragments. TV clips and news broadcasts are also incorporated, overlapped in a broken and sped-up manner with Rocha's interventions and Lessa's own voice (which resurfaces here and there). Furthermore, what could at first appear as a series of traces inscribed at some personal level is complicated by other materials added to the film triptych, and subjected to a methodical theatricalization.

The changes in medium – of what began as an occupation project and became a documentary triptych – activate, necessarily, other layers of materials, variations, and contrapositions. The fundamental elements, throughout the triptych, are both the fragments from Rocha's films and the bits of speech taken from his interventions and interviews, as well as contemporary artworks sharply illuminated by Rocha's aesthetics. In each series of contrapositions and speculative-imagetic echoes – dystopia / utopia, commodity / reification, extinction / reasons to "keep on keeping on" – we hear voices interrupting other voices, figures overlapped with other figures, choruses against choruses, and piles and piles of different kinds of accumulations. Inside every zone of choralization, infrachoruses contrast with other infrachoruses, and there is no cohesion sustaining simple, opposing pairs, because pairs act as mutual folds.

Even the figures that move through the urban landscape in the first episode of the triptych (predominantly mourning and dystopic) are themselves geminations. The bodies that appear in the triptych (in the first one, most of all) are composite bodies, made with fragments of things and pieces of other bodies, their faces evincing the extraction of each different fragment that composes them. These figures deliberately recall, at times, the photomontages of Greta Stern, both because of their composite nature and due to the strident explicitness of their cutouts, an explicitness that is maintained throughout the triptych.

The last segment of the triptych contrasts different city and community projects conceived and discussed throughout Brazil in the years before Lessa's project was completed. Even in this part of the triptych (where people making the case for these projects finely contradict each other), speech is kept inconclusive by Lessa. What seems most pressing in the films is the intense flux and the continuous activation of recombined elements. Certain images and speech excerpts return repeatedly, and they interact with each other at the same time as different areas of reflection, different hypotheses of fabulation, get drawn. The uninterrupted presentation of materials stops short of being an organized collection, with everything in its right place, and at the same time it does not shy away from rearticulations. Geminated structures in the film triptych thus function in a way that keeps the act of recombination potentially active.

Lessa's film triptych was made between 2020 and 2022. In 2022, the films were shown online, and that same year the exhibition space of the SESC in Avenida Paulista reopened. The pre-filmed triptych was blown up to immense scale and screened almost on a loop, in continuous enlarged projection throughout the day. Lessa's choice of film as medium gained contrast and refiguration with the return to in-person activities after the pandemic. Thanks to the in-person screening of the films – which the artist referred to as an exhibition manifesto – the *documentary-manifesto* (the film triptych) found itself paired with live performances and printing actions (different images and speeches from videos shown on site were printed also on site, using sophisticated printing devices). In this way, yet another choral dynamic was constituted, amidst the chain of reconfigurations feeding into and out of Lessa's triptych. Based on the guiding notion of a manifesto, one language (film) is, then, confronted with another one (performance), and then with another one (on-site interventions), in a dynamic where one language constantly confronts and supplements the other (Figure 8).

The initial spirit of occupation of Lessa's project was then, at first, redirected to film editing. Later, the sequence of films itself was redefined by the inclusion of theatricalized snippets. One more refiguration took place as a response to yet another interpellation. As Lessa's films were being screened at the SESC in Avenida Paulista, while live performances were taking place, and once images and speech from her films began to be printed using printers on site, acts and objects spawned as part of this assemblage of film, performance, and printing were taken out of the exhibition space and into the street. Lessa, other artists present, and the audience itself brought the project into confrontation with an out-of-frame, an off-field: the street itself. The performances at SESC in Avenida Paulista started to occupy a space beyond the exhibition rooms, incorporating weekend activities taking place in the street and the comings and goings of Avenida Paulista. The initial project, then, unfolded twice, into a kind of triple fabulation: from (unrealized) occupation project to film triptych, from film triptych to exhibition and performance, and from exhibition and performance into a kind of flash-protest.

8 Photograph from Bia Lessa's own archive, which captures the performance-protests that took place during the occupation-exhibition linked to her project *Cartas ao mundo*, organized by the artist in 2022 in SESC Avenida Paulista, in São Paulo.

The Off-Field

The street is a fundamental element in the project of occupation of Largo de Paissandu, in the clips from Rocha's films, and it erupts once again, in an active form, in the flash protests that emerge from the exhibition version of Lessa's triptych. The discarded targets from shooting ranges have, as we have seen, a determinant role in Barros' video titled *Alvos*, and they frame the three-dimensional drawings shown in the exhibition *Pisa na paúra* by the same artist. These targets were found by the artist as trash discarded on the streets, usually close to shooting clubs.

Since 2018, Nuno Ramos has been systematically working with interferences and dissents between field and off-field in a series of performances that he calls, generically, *Aos vivos*, a double entendre, equally signaling the living (addressing the act to whoever is alive, and, somewhat, summoning them), live TV programs (which he mentions and follows in some performances), and live presentations such as the two versions of *A gente se vê por aqui* (2017 and 2018),[58] the three works titled *Aos vivos: Debates*[59] (2018), and *Dito e feito*[60] (2021).

His usual method employs insertions, calculated insertions (with a brief time delay, and in a different context) of a text that originated in some audiovisual off-field: television (electoral debates, programming from TV Globo), films (*Terra em transe*, 1967), video (conversations recorded in the streets in *Dito e feito*). The reference text and the context of reinsertion are previously announced, and repetition happens, then, in real time, through audios shared using headphones.

Contrary to what generally takes place, for example, in the plays by the Wooster Group[61] (which tend to visually expose their referents when they conduct differential re-enactments), the performances conceived by Nuno Ramos allow viewers to know, but not necessarily see, the source of the repetitions shared through headphones. Viewers also know that the audio comes, sequentially and instantaneously, with a short time gap, from a context outside the performance frame. And these works construct themselves rhythmically from the vacillations, from the hesitations, from the delays between transmission and retransmission, audio and scenic action, frame and outside-the-frame.

Along with Eduardo Climachauska, Ramos adopted a similar procedure (but based on a different proposition) in *Cassandra 1*, a performance that took place in Galeria Anita Schwartz on June 9, 2018, from 12 p.m. to 6 p.m. In that case, the outside-the-frame was offered by an issue of the newspaper *O Globo* published that same day and read by both artists, with their heads turned toward the walls of the gallery, their backs to the public, and refraining from any interaction with it. The reading was continuous until they, suddenly, came across some indicative expression of time or duration. When that happened, a brief interruption took place and it was immediately registered in a kind of chronometer. They then returned to the newspaper and to registering the passage of time.

In 2022, in a reading/performance/installation titled *Perdido* (Figure 9), that continuous form of reading was kept, but with a significant alteration in the place attributed to the off-field (which no longer provides the text read during the performance) and with a pluralization of the acoustic vantage points. In this case, the performance consisted in a complete reading of Proust's *In Search of Lost Time* at the Biblioteca Municipal Mário de Andrade, a project which lasted for 21 days, for 8 hours each day. Most of the reading was played on speakers submerged in seven aquariums, each one with a spectator-fish. Over the course of the reading, each time that the word "time" appeared in the text, the reader performing at that moment would repeat the word into another microphone, connected to a speaker installed in Consolação Street. At the same time, a motorcycle driver

9 Photograph of the reading/installation/performance titled *Perdido* (2022) by Nuno Ramos. The reading/installation/performance was streamed live during its 21-day run, and it took place at the Biblioteca Municipal Mário de Andrade in São Paulo.

moving through the streets of São Paulo was notified, and he was previously instructed to immediately scream "time" using a megaphone, regardless of where he was.

In that series of performances by Ramos, the "live" convocation of the out-of-the-frame is presented as a segmentation of times (however concomitant) and as the pairing-in-discord of contexts (not all of them visually available, of course). It is presented either as an information source, or as a listening place, or as the place of its repercussion. What is underlined, then, with the urgency of real time, is a scission not just in enunciation, in the emitting source (which is linked to audios or to other sources), but in the very awareness of the insertion of the performer and the observer in shared time, in common life, which also lag. The contrast, even if minimal, the lag, even if negligible, in those repetitions, emphasize the split between those contexts, those contemporaneities, in so far as they are active and co-present. The temporal segmentations impose, from that point of view, a necessarily split experience of the present hour.

In *Extraquadro*,[62] a book published by Editora Impressões de Minas in 2021, Ricardo Aleixo points directly to a similar reinforcement of the function of the off-field. The very title chosen by the author signals this, of course, but so do the use of intervals, the empty spaces, the intra-page parallel columns, the layout that almost bleeds out of the margins (Figure 10), the internal expansions between the poems. Two minimal fragments ("all the time // and now"[63]) from the poem that lends its name to the book, for example, unfold beautifully into multiple variations of a statement that functions as the title of another poem – "O tempo todo tudo muda"[64] ("The whole time everything changes"). The sentence occupies the body of the poem and keeps repeating and recombining itself, thus producing almost imperceptible infra-distinctions, finishing the poem with a slight rephrasing: "Everything changes the whole time."

In that sense, *Extraquadro* engages with the poet's entire trajectory, with his reinventions – through performance, through cutouts of his own poems in new vocalizations, through topical textual variations, and through acoustic and musical experimentations. In the 2021 book, however, Aleixo seems to engage in a particularly intense dialogue with *Impossível como nunca ter tido um rosto* from 2016.

Impossível como nunca ter tido um rosto presents an almost programmatic exposition of different forms of reframing and hollowing out the poem. In "Rosto" ("Face"), for instance, the whole hypothesis of figuration is undermined by the use of parentheses, some of which are intentionally dislocated, some turned inside out, pointing to the poem's own silence, its uncertainty, signaling a possible unfolding, a displacement, a false impression. Even at the end of the poem, when a possible image is imagined, and a figuration is almost announced, impossibility remains: ") The possible face, given the / circumstances (/ Impossible as never having had a face)". Another poem – "The Only Things" – deals with what is "between," what slides between things. It grapples with the interval of transformation, the interruption of a movement, what "exists and nobody sees / nor hears this // that exists. / This". The text itself is self-defined as this "that is between," as an almost off-screen space that cuts across the frame and presents itself as a fold, as an inside/outside. This is also summarized in "Timbre": "everything passed / in intervals blows / from tense wings // timbre that / resounds in the vacuum of // zero / to one" ("tudo passado / a intervalos golpes / de asas tensas // timbre que / retine no vácuo do // zero / ao um").

These procedures – the methodical investigation of the interval-fold, of graphic interruptions, of silence, and of forms of the cut and the cutout – also guide Aleixo in *Extraquadro*. The book, as the poem "Passagens" (metapoetically) states, is a "rumor / of images / some against / other ones / some close / to the other ones / some inside / the other ones / some."[65] With an explicit focus on the tension between frame and outside-the-frame, we see, in *Extraquadro,* a new series of parenthetical experiments (in "Mim mesmo," "Mecânica popular," "À tua espera," "Sem chão," "A recusa da musa"), of interval leaks ("Quase épico," "Programa"), of spacing ("Aquele por quem esperavam"), and of interruptions ("Me dis," "Mesmo qu"). We also see direct thematizations of silence (as in "Meu corpo"), and of a dramatized scission of the voice (see "Igual como?" and "Houve casos em que o passado veio mais de uma vez").

In *Extraquadro*, there is a very particular form of refiguration of that interval poetics, and of those tensions that inhabit the graphic space of the poems. And there is also an out-of-frame of a whole different order that is literally exposed in the book (through a real and an imaginary photograph). In the opening

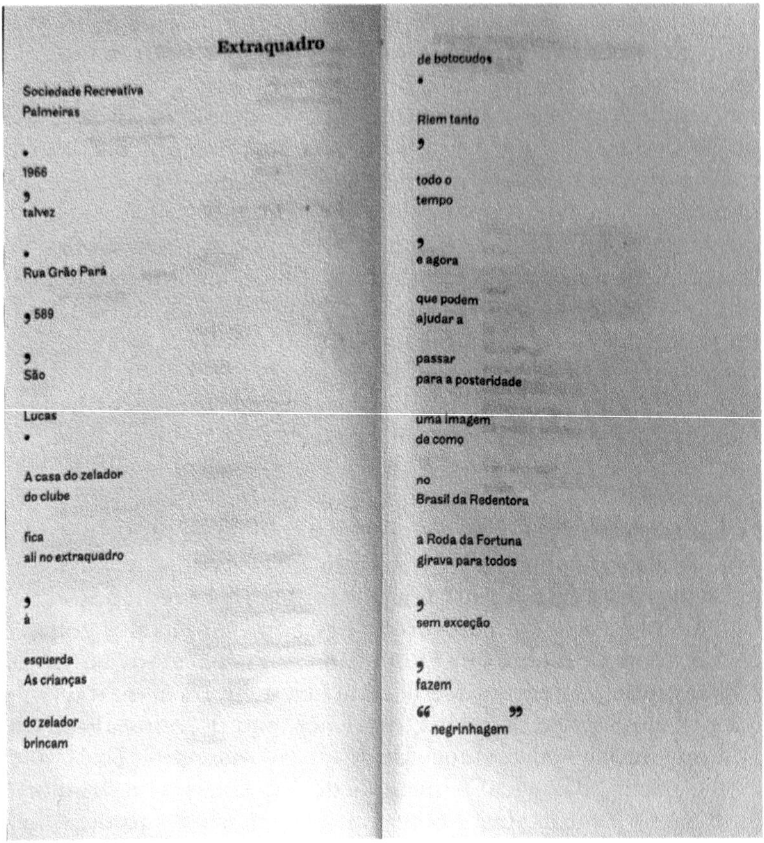

Extraquadro

Sociedade Recreativa
Palmeiras

•
1966
,
talvez

•
Rua Grão Pará

, 589

,
São

Lucas
•

A casa do zelador
do clube

fica
ali no extraquadro

,
à

esquerda
As crianças

do zelador
brincam

de botocudos
•

Riem tanto
,

todo o
tempo

,
e agora

que podem
ajudar a

passar
para a posteridade

uma imagem
de como

no
Brasil da Redentora

a Roda da Fortuna
girava para todos

,
sem exceção

,
fazem
“ negrinhagem ”

10 Photographic reproduction of the poem titled “Extraquadro” (2020) by Ricardo Aleixo, published in a book by the same name. The layout of the poem is important because it shows a deliberate graphic concentration toward the page margins, as if the poem was running away toward the space beyond the frame.

poem of the book, “Quase épico” (“Almost Epic”), for example, Aleixo invents a nonexistent photo exposing the elegant bravery of his father and his uncle promenading, in the 1920s, through Praça da Liberdade, in Belo Horizonte, on a walk “reserved for whites.” In the poem “Extraquadro,” what’s at stake is also a photo, in this case a real one, as well as some exclusions offered by means of some out-of-frame spaces.

“Extraquadro” is fundamentally a description of that photograph. It has an address (Rua Grão Pará, 589), a location (São

Lucas), and a caption (Sociedade Recreativa Palmeiras); its date is undetermined (1966, perhaps), and part of the group of children pictured playing in it is identified (the children of the building custodian). The photograph is included in the book's back cover, almost hidden, placed under its dust jacket. But the reader is almost ironically given a kind of certificate of truth. The photo is intentionally there, but the reproduction is, intentionally, not particularly clear. Meanwhile, the poem makes the following clear: the photograph in itself is, and it is not, the out-of-frame. It leaves us, then, with the expectation of – and a discreet reference to – yet another off-field issue.

The photo (as described) exposes, in it, the exclusion (in the framing) of the custodian's house – and that's why all you see is a club. The photo also pictures laughter and, at the same time, it does not expose the grief of Brazil under military dictatorship, an absent grief that keeps haunting the photo. The image organizes all the children around the same "circle," while racism, social inequality, and political authoritarianism encircled (almost invisibly) this same circle.

But we read distinctly that the scene has a context – the "Brazil of the Redentora" ("Redeemer" was how the Brazilian military referred to the 1964 coup, and how it is referred to now by those nostalgic for the dictatorship). The choice of this expression by the poet, the appearance of it, almost whisper-like, makes it even more menacing, as if the military presence was once again perceivably close – the way it was, in fact, in Brazil in 2021. All this constitutes a particular kind of out-of-frame, as political as the discreet but unequivocal references to race and inequality in the poem. Aleixo layers this contextual out-of-the-frame onto the other components of the poem, the same way he does, in different ways, in poems such as "Rondó da ronda noturna," "Meu negro," "Conheço vocês pelo cheiro," "Brancos," among others. He thus imposes it as a decisive factor in the composition of the poem.

The emphasis on the out-of-the-frame in Aleixo's book from 2021; the move to the streets of the flash protests spawned by the exhibition version of Bia Lessa's *Cartas ao mundo*; the discarded targets used at a shooting range and then repurposed as exhibition material by Lenora de Barros; the *motoboy* yelling "Time" as he drives through the streets of downtown São Paulo in Nuno Ramos' *Perdido* – all this brings to the fore an almost raw presence of the historical hour in artistic and critical experience.

Returning, once again, to Silviano Santiago's fable, and to the overdeveloped parasitic network through which the Brazilian situation during the ultra-right expansion is considered here, it is evident now that this picturing was not at all fortuitous. As Victor Klemperer registered in his study on the language of the Third Reich cited elsewhere in this book, it's worth noting how habitual it was, in Nazi Germany, to refer to Jewish peoples as the "parasitic race," deriving from this racist, injurious association a whole set of negative expressions, which relate, furthermore, to the acts of extermination undertaken by the Reich. Examples of this are the name given to a home guard instituted toward the end of World War II (the "Combat Team Against the Parasites of the People"), and the name of the enterprise directly responsible for the shipment of lethal gas to the extermination camps (the "International Combat Society Against Parasites").

In the early days of Bolsonaro's government, the Minister of the Economy, Paulo Guedes, also tried, unsuccessfully, to link parasites to Brazilian public servants. Bolsonarista groups and aligned social networks used the media to try to do the same through a constant assault on artists, intellectuals, social movements, unhoused and landless people, *quilombolas*, indigenous people, research grant recipients, and so forth. Invariably re-emerging in those hate choruses – as the work on hate speeches by Giselle Beiguelman shows – is the expression "parasite" as a qualifier or diagnosis that signals exclusion. In neither case (the case of the minister, and the case of the digital fascist choruses), did the strategy (similar to the one adopted by the Nazi leadership) succeed at the scale desired by those agents of the ultra-right.

On the contrary, and not so paradoxically, the analogy to parasitism would gain applicability and relevance, over the course of the last few years and as I tried to note here, when the objects named by that expression were the Bolsonaro government itself, the colonies of dysfunctional figures embedded in different public institutions during his administration, and the economic policies of dismantlement, on a large scale, of everything that was supposed to be public. This perception was forcibly expanded with the disarray during the pandemic, with the coronavirus (an intracellular parasite), and with the thousands of deaths caused by this virus, gesturing, involuntarily and mournfully, to the immediate consequences of the Bolsonaro regime that rose to power after the 2016 coup.

This situation was confronted by artistic and literary interventions that, intentionally elaborating the image of "hosts," or acting sometimes as "hosts" themselves, invented other (intensely critical) forms of non-parasitic duplication. In this sense, they activated different procedures of critical coupling and gemination, and compositional dynamics driven by material awareness, variation, and methodical disagreement. They never worked by assimilation or vicarious presence. These are cultural works that are not, and do not intend to be, simple mimetic responses to the references with which they explicitly interact. Nor do they act by literally imitating the social context that gave rise to them.

Meanwhile, as we have observed here, these cultural manifestations and artistic projects offer, in this context and in these interactions, a contrasting framework endowed with a singular deconstructive potency. They possess a kind of undeniable practical quality, as they affirm, in circumstances of sometimes aporetic semi-paralysis, crucial forms of autonomy. In this sense, let us return to the concluding passages of "Ovos de marimbondo" – inclement and undetermined, highlighting the fearsome efficacy of the parasite. This book, then, lands, once again, in a context of active confrontation, in Brazil and beyond its borders. It points, most of all, to the radicality that gave shape to the dynamics of dissension activated by these artistic experiments.

Notes

1 Regarding the Chorus

1 Two texts by Martin Mégevand were particularly relevant as references for some of the essays brought together in this book: Martin Mégevand, "L'éternel retour du chœur," in "Masques, intertextes," *Littérature* 131, 2003: 105–22; "Chœur et choralité dans le théâtre de la décolonisation: les exemples de Kateb Yacine et d'Aimé Césaire," *Cahiers de l'Association internationale des études françaises* 46, 1994: 231–41.

2 It is evidently impossible not to think of Mikhail Bakhtin when it comes to polyphony. It is important to remember, on the other hand, his borrowings from Menippean satire, from popular theater, from the *commedia dell'arte*, his attribution of an incorrigible monologic, monocomposed character to drama. See his remarks included in *Problems of Dostoevsky's Poetics*. Bakhtin's link to the theater has been the subject of many studies and the critical discussion of his view of theater demands a more expansive, comprehensive study.

3 Christophe Triau, "Choralités diffractées: la communauté en creux," *Alternatives théâtrales. Choralités* 76–7 (2003): 5–11.

4 Antônio Cândido, *O discurso e a cidade* (São Paulo: Duas Cidades, 1993): 152.

5 André Lepecki, "Coreopolítica e coreopolícia," *ILHA* 13.1: 42–60. See Lepecki, *Exhausting Dance: Performance and the Politics of Movement* (New York: Routledge, 2006).

6 In this regard, see Hans-Thies Lehmann, *Tragedia y teatro dramático* (Mexico City: Paso de Gato, 2017). Lehmann's book and other

studies more directly focused on the theater chorus (such as those by Claude Calame, Gregory Nagy, Deborah Tarn Steiner, Joshua Billings) are analyzed in an essay that is not included in this book.

7 See Nicole Loraux, "La tragédie Grecque: théâtre engagé ou Oratoire," in *La Voix endeuillée. Essai sur la tragédie grecque* (Paris: Gallimard / NRF Essais,1999): 9–27.

8 After pressure from the church, he was pardoned in 1972, but the year after that, Georges Glaeser presented a complaint against him at Lyon, accusing him of crimes against humanity. He would not be imprisoned until May 24, 1989. He was found guilty of crimes against humanity and condemned to life in prison, where he would die from cancer in 1996.

9 In his interview, as published in the magazine *L'Express*, Darquier maintained that the gas chambers at Auschwitz were used to treat lice, and that allegations of mass killings at that camp were fabrications created and disseminated by Jews. Darquier was exiled in Spain, where he lived under the protection of the Franco regime. France requested his extradition, but this request was never granted.

10 Nicole Loraux talks about this in "Elogio do anacronismo," in Adauto Novaes, ed., *Tempo e História* (São Paulo: Companhia das Letras, 1992).

11 These *Jornadas* are evoked explicitly in works by André Vallias and Grace Passô analyzed elsewhere in this book.

2 Dissonant Choralities (and the Context of the 2013 *Jornadas de Junho*)

1 In June 2013, a movement, known as the June Days, filled Brazilian streets with protesters, led initially by the Free Fare Movement (MPL) and motivated at first by a 20 percent increase to public transport fares, but also by various other factors linked to everyday life in metropolitan areas – the precariousness of the labor market, the time spent on public transport, the employment and payment prospects that did not keep pace with the democratization of education led by the Workers' Party governments. The violent police repression fueled public rage, and a series of dissatisfactions and movements gained visibility, which included not only the growing demand for representation of groups historically underrepresented in positions of power – indigenous people, Black people, women, and the LGBTQI+ community – but also right-wing and far-right groups nostalgic for the military dictatorship and eager to undermine left-wing parties and pave their own return to power.

2 José Celso Martinez Corrêa, "Roda Viva: energia milenar no coro aqui e agora," in "Blog do Zé Celso": https://goo.gl/Xjt7YX.
3 For a video of this work by the Coletivo Improviso, see: https://vimeo.com/413392380?fl=pl&fe=sh.
4 "Objets verbaux non identifiés," an expression originally coined by Pierre Alferi and Olivier Cadiot, but whose critical unfolding, realized by Christophe Hanna in *Nos dispositifs poétiques*, is what interests me here. See Cristophe Hanna, *Nos dispositifs poétiques* (Paris: Questions Théoriques, 2010).
5 "Comentário, na rede, sobre tudo o que está acontecendo por aí."
6 Hanna, *Nos dispositifs poétiques.*
7 Luiz Ruffato, "Viver de literatura," *O Globo* (Sept. 1, 2013: https://oglobo.globo.com/cultura/viver-de-literatura-9777435.
8 See Rosana Lobo's review of Regina Dalcastagnè's new book: *O Globo* (Oct. 20, 2012): https://glo.bo/2hb4jHI.
9 Leyla Perrone-Moisés, "A literatura exigente," *Folha de São Paulo, Ilustríssima* (March 25, 2012): https://www1.folha.uol.com.br/fsp/ilustrissima/33216-a-literatura-exigente.shtml.
10 Ferreira, *As visitas que hoje estamos* (São Paulo: Iluminuras, 2012).
11 "Rush" can be downloaded here: https://www4.pucsp.br/revistafronteiraz/numeros_anteriores/n1/download/RUSH_2.pdf.
12 In André Sant'Anna, *Sexo e amizade* (São Paulo: Companhia das Letras, 2007).
13 The short novel *Sexo* was originally published in 1999 by Editora 7 Letras.
14 See Ramos' website: www.nunoramos.com.br/trabalhos.

3 Artistic Actions / Political Actions (Before and After Rousseff's Impeachment)

1 What came after was the Temer and Bolsonaro administrations, inflation, frozen investments in the areas of health and education, disruption of workers' organizations, loss of labor rights and income, rising costs, and food insecurity.
2 The poem and accompanying photograph can be found here: https://revistamododeusar.blogspot.com/search?q=berkeley. Angélica Freitas was one of the magazine's editors, together with the poets Marília Garcia and Ricardo Domeneck. The online publication shut down in 2017.
3 In Portuguese: "Carga de Cavalaria, com espadas em punho, pelo 4° Regimento de Polícia Montada."
4 It is worth remembering that on May 12, 2016, the Brazilian Senate

approved the opening of the impeachment process, removing Dilma from the presidency until the process was concluded.

5 I have previously written about the emergence, and some of the returns-in-difference, of songs of exile in Brazilian literature – among other essays, in "Brito Broca and the Theme of Homecoming in Brazilian Romanticism" (*Revista Remate de Males* 11, 1991: 89–102): https://doi.org/10.20396/remate.v11i1.8635956.

6 "Eu é um rinoceronte um hipopótamo – / de repente eu estava em todos os lugares / em todos os lugares / e numa caixa … ."

7 In Franklin Alves Dassie, *Grandes mamíferos* (Rio de Janeiro: 7 Letras, 2016).

8 For more on Alice Miceli's Projeto Chernobyl, see www.alicemiceli.com/projects/chernobyl.

9 See www.premiopipa.com/pag/artistas/lais-myrrha.

10 This is a reference to two verses from Lu Menezes' "Fontes de Renda" series, where, at a certain point, there is another beautiful reinterpretation – on a micro-scale – of the opposition between here and there that characterizes the songs of exile: "O fato é que no 'esquema' em pauta / um lugar qualquer do globo terrestre / coincidiria com um ponto do bordado. / O lá se converteria em cá, o ali em aqui / no bastidor de alguma mulher / que a cada ponto a cada instante / seu e de tudo – *aprenderia / o quê? além do preciso / presente impreciso / dela no mundo?*" ("The fact is that in the 'scheme' in question / any place on the globe / would coincide with a point in the embroidery / The there would become the here, therein would become herein / in the embroidery hoop of some woman / who, with each stitch, each instant / hers and everything else's / – would learn / what? besides the precise / imprecise present of her in the world?"). See Lu Menezes and Augusto Massi, *Gabinete de curiosidades* (São Paulo: Luna Parque, 2016): 27. Translation by Flora Süssekind.

11 See https://revistausina.com/2014/08/16/entrevista-com-joana-cesar.

12 "… o que foi usado não precisa / ser reciclado encadernado como novo / o que vem do uso carece ser / ocupado reescrito como o primeiro livro / de um gênero curioso exposto à fratura / em conjuntura de crise que nada finda / ou apenas isso um desejo de mundo."

13 In Dassie, *Grandes mamíferos*.

14 See Augusto de Campos, *Despoesia* (São Paulo: Perspectiva, 1994).

15 See "Livro do cão – 1," in Carlito Azevedo, *Livro das postagens* (Rio de Janeiro: 7 letras, 2016).

16 Carlito Azevedo, "Prólogo canino-operístico," in *Livro das postagens*: "com todos os outros / gotas de suor / rolando da testa / batidas mais rápidas / no peito / quando a bala /vara o cubo / quando as bombas explodem / explodem / reduzem o cubo / a pó."

4 Negative Epiphanies

1 2019 was the first year of Bolsonaro's ultra-right government in Brazil.
2 A color version of the poem can be found here: www.instagram.com/p/B3osDdbHEWI.
3 It can be seen at: https://fotografia.folha.uol.com.br/galerias/1650199637146516-cildo-meireles-publica-imagem-misteriosa-em-reportagem-da-folha.
4 "Mineirinho," in Clarice Lispector, *A legião estrangeira* (Rio de Janeiro: Editora do Autor, 1964).
5 Roland Barthes, *The Pleasure of the Text*, trans. Richard Miller (New York: Hill and Wang, 1975): 4.
6 Roland Barthes, *O prazer do texto*, trans. J. Guinsburg (São Paulo: Editora Perspectiva, 1987): 8.
7 See Ana Cristina Cesar, *Crítica e tradução* (São Paulo: Companhia das Letras, 2016).
8 Katherine Mansfield, *Bliss, and Other Stories* (New York: A. A. Knopf, 1922): 135.
9 Ana Cristina Cesar, *Inéditos e dispersos: poesia/prosa*, ed. and trans. Armando Freitas Filho (São Paulo: Brasiliense, 1985).
10 Mansfield, *Bliss*, 123.
11 Cesar, *Crítica e tradução*.
12 See João Camillo Penna, "O nu de Clarice Lispector," *Alea* 12.1 (2010).
13 Clarice Lispector, *Água Viva* (1973; Rio de Janeiro: Rocco, 2009): 4.
14 In Clarice Lispector, *Laços de família* (1960; Rio de Janeiro: Rocco, 1998).
15 Luiz Eduardo Soares, *O Brasil e seu duplo* (São Paulo: Todavia, 2019).
16 Davi Arrigucci Jr., *O cacto e as ruínas: a poesia entre outras artes* (São Paulo: Duas Cidades / Editora 34, 2000): 17.
17 Manuel Bandeira, "The Creature," in *This Earth, That Sky: Poems by Manuel Bandeira*, trans. Candace Slater (Berkeley: University of California Press, 1989): 183.
18 The Portuguese version of this essay can be read here: https://pernambucorevista.com.br/acervo/pernambuco/93-especial/1742-a%C3%A7%C3%B5es-pol%C3%ADticas,-a%C3%A7%C3%B5es-art%C3%ADsticas.html.
19 "Adam's Curse," a poem that was later rewritten and mixed with another one in his 2025 book *Vida: efeito-V* (Rio de Janeiro: 7 Letras, 2025).
20 In Carlito Azevedo, *Livro das postagens* (Rio de Janeiro: 7 Letras, 2016).

21 "A via-láctea se despenteia. / Os corpos se gastam contra a luz. / Sem artifícios, a pedra / acende sua mancha sobre a praia. / Do lixo da esquina partiu / o último voo da varejeiracontra um século convulsivo."
22 "Era bonito ver / à noite / da janela de casa / ou da mureta / da praia / o estaleiro / envolto na / aura de suas / próprias luzes / sobrepostas, / soldas, maçaricos, / refletores, holofotes, / luminárias pendentes, / arcos voltaicos, / relâmpagos / sem nenhuma / tempestade."
23 "Alguém que você / nunca viu / corre desesperadamente / em sua direção; / alguém ou alguma / aparição do reino / do luto e da tragédia; / alguém como uma / contradição antagônica / num mar de / contradições / não-antagônicas; / alguém se afogando / na ganga mística / da avenida no ocaso; / alguém em cujas / esponjas cerebrais / jamais se fundariam / as bases inabaláveis / de um sólido império; / alguém que necessita / a qualquer custo / falar com você; / mas você é tão distraído / entra no carro / ou no cinema / ou no elevador / escapa sem nem / saber que escapa / do rodamoinho / no fundo / do caldeirão de / feiticeira / da história."
24 Marcel Duchamp, "Projets," in *Notes* (Paris: Flammarion, 1999): 115.
25 Pierre Cabanne, *Marcel Duchamp: Engenheiro do tempo perdido* (São Paulo: Perspectiva, 2008).
26 Reyes Mate, *Meia-noite na história, comentários às teses de W. Benjamin "Sobre o conceito de História"* (São Leopoldo: Editora Unisinos, 2011): 211.

5 Critical Grammars of the Middle Classes

1 Nathalie Quintane, "Le suicide des classes moyennes," in *Les Années 10* (Paris: La Fabrique Éditions, 2014): 165–74.
2 Nathalie Quintane, *Que faire des classes moyennes?* (Paris: P. O. L. Éditeur, 2016).
3 Vilma Arêas, *Um beijo por mês* (São Paulo: Luna Parque, 2018).
4 These are the books by Veronica Stigger mentioned in this chapter: *Gran Cabaret Demenzial* (São Paulo: Cosac Naify, 2007); *Os anões* (São Paulo: Cosac Naify, 2010); *Delírio de damasco* (Florianópolis: Cultura e Barbárie, Desterro, 2012); and *Sul* (São Paulo: Editora 34, 2016).
5 Roberto Schwarz, "Orelha para Francisco Alvim," in *Sequências brasileiras* (São Paulo: Companhia das Letras, 1999): 205–6.
6 Roland Barthes, *Aula*, trans. Leyla Perrone-Moisés (São Paulo: Cultrix, 1989).
7 Jacques Rancière. "O inesquecível," in *Figuras da história* (São Paulo: Editora da UNESP, 2018): 21.

8 Berta Waldman, "A narrativa de Dalton Trevisan: um pedaço bruto de vida," in *Ensaios sobre a obra de Dalton Trevisan* (Campinas: Editora da UNICAMP, 2014): 161–70.
9 Clarice Lispector, *The Hour of the Star*, trans. Benjamin Moser (New York: New Directions, 2020): 10.
10 Ibid., 7.
11 Ibid., 4.
12 Ibid., 22.
13 See Clarice Lispector, *Todas as cartas* (Rio de Janeiro: Rocco Digital, 2020): 384.
14 See *Rascunho* 151, Nov. 1, 2012: https://rascunho.com.br/paiol-literario/francisco-alvim.
15 Ibid.
16 Émile Benveniste, "Estrutura da língua e estrutura da sociedade," in *Problemas de linguística geral II* (Campinas: Pontes, 2006): 102.
17 Dalton Trevisan, *234 ministórias* (Rio de Janeiro: Editora Record, 1997).
18 Vilma Arêas, "Jogo de contrários," in Francisco Alvim, *Elefante* (Lisbon: Cotovia / Ângelus Novus, 2004).
19 Valêncio Xavier Niculitcheff (1933–2008) is the author of, among other books, *O mez da grippe e outros livros* (São Paulo: Companhia das Letras,1999); *Desembrulhando as balas Zequinha* (Curitiba: Payol, 1973); *Meu sétimo dia – novela-rebus* (São Paulo: Ciências do Acidente, 1998); *Minha mãe morrendo* e *menino mentido* (São Paulo: Companhia das Letras, 2001).
20 Silviano Santiago, *Crescendo durante a guerra numa província ultramarina* (Rio de Janeiro: Livraria F. Alves Editora, 1978); *O falso mentiroso: memórias* (Rio de Janeiro: Rocco, 2004).
21 See Judith Butler, "Adotando o ponto de vista do outro: implicações ambivalentes" in Axel Honneth, *Reificação: Um estudo de teoria do reconhecimento* (São Paulo: Editora UNESP, 2018): 137.
22 "Um menino preto, de carne e osso, e uma estátua branca de pedra."
23 The series of texts titled "Instantâneo" can be found in Arêas, *Um beijo por mês*.
24 Veronica Stigger, *O trágico e outras comédias* (Rio de Janeiro: 7Letras, 2004).
25 In Veronica Stigger, *Os anões* (São Paulo, Cosac Naify, 2010): 6-12.
26 José de Souza Martins, "O lado sombrio da mente conservadora" (1996) in *Linchamentos: A justiça popular no Brasil* (São Paulo: Editora Contexto, 2019): 88.
27 Ibid., 72.
28 Martins, "O lado sombrio da mente conservadora," 3.
29 See Flora Süssekind and Tânia Dias (eds.), *Cultura brasileira hoje: Diálogos*, vol. II (Rio de Janeiro: Fundação Casa de Rui Barbosa,

2018): 53. The book can be downloaded at www.academia.edu/40870727/volume_2_CULTURA_BRASILEIRA_HOJE_DI%C3%81LOGOS.

30 In André Sant'Anna, *Sexo e amizade* (São Paulo: Companhia das Letras, 2007).

31 André Sant'Anna's "A lei" can be accessed at https://rascunho.com.br/ficcao-e-poesia/a-lei.

32 Süssekind and Dias, *Cultura brasileira hoje*, 45.

33 André Sant'Anna, *Discurso sobre a metástase* (São Paulo: Todavia, 2021).

34 André Sant'Anna, *O Brasil é bom* (São Paulo: Companhia das Letras, 2014).

35 Ibid.

36 Judith Butler, *Frames of War: When Is Life Grievable?* (Verso: London, 2016): 12.

6 Choruses Against Counter-Choruses

1 Jacques Derrida, "Le retrait de la métaphore," in *Psyché. Inventions de l'autre*, vol. I (Paris: Galilée, 1987): 105.

2 The reference here is to an observation Aristotle makes in Book VII of his *Poetics*: "A beautiful object, whether it be a picture of a living organism or any whole composed of parts, must not only have an orderly arrangement of parts, but must also be of a certain magnitude; for beauty depends on magnitude and order." See *The Poetics of Aristotle*, ed. and trans. S. H. Butcher (New York: The McMillan Company, 1902): 31.

3 Nuno Ramos, "Sai Antígona," *Revista Piauí* 167 (August 2020): https://piaui.folha.uol.com.br/materia/sai-antigona.

4 Silviano Santiago, "Ovos de marimbondo, uma fábula," *Suplemento Pernambuco*, July 25, 2020. See: https://suplementopernambuco.com.br/edi%C3%A7%C3%B5es-anteriores/2522-ovos-de-marimbondo,-uma-f%C3%A1bula.html.

5 Alvos' video can be viewed at: https://youtu.be/ZRxFbgTMplQ?si=S2P0ArJoZi9_INa2.

6 See Bárbara Silveira and Felipe Paranhos, "Sobre temer no poder, Dilma vê 'parasita' que 'se continuar, mata a democracia.'" This article was published by UOL and republished in *Metro 1* on June 28, 2016: www.metro1.com.br/noticias/politica/18647,sobre-temer-no-poder-dilma-ve-parasita-que-se-continuar-mata-a-democracia.

7 Theodor W. Adorno, *Aspects of the New Right-Wing Extremism*, trans. Wieland Hoban (Cambridge: Polity, 2020): 5.

8 See Marcos Nobre, "O vírus e o parasita," *Ilustríssima, Folha de*

São Paulo (March 18, 2020). The online version can be accessed at: www1.folha.uol.com.br/ilustrissima/2020/03/e-preciso-por-bolsonaro-emquarentena-para-superar-crise-do-coronavirus.shtml.

9 Ibid.

10 See Karl Marx, *The Civil War in France* (New York: International Publishers, 1962).

11 See Rosa Luxemburg, *The Accumulation of Capital*, trans. Agnes Schwarzschild (London: Routledge, 2003). In addition, see Isabel Loureiro, "A menos eurocêntrica de todos: Rosa Luxemburgo e a acumulação primitiva permanente," in *Rosa Luxemburgo: ou o preço da Liberdade*, ed. Jörn Schütrumpf (São Paulo: Fundação Rosa Luxemburgo, 2015): 97–107.

12 See Manoel Bomfim, *A América Latina: males de origem. O parasitismo social e evolução* (Rio de Janeiro: Garnier, [1905]).

13 In Zygmunt Bauman, *History and Politics: Selected Writings*, vol. II (Cambridge: Polity Press, 2023): 178–85.

14 Ibid.

15 Márcio Pochmann, "Brasil, vitrine do rentismo parasitário," *Outras Palavras* (November 16, 2021): https://outraspalavras.net/desigualdades-mundo/pochmann-brasilvitrine-do-rentismo-parasitario.

16 Rodrigo Nunes does not explicitly use parasitism analogies in this article. But the analogy emerged in an interview with João Vitor Santos on February 15, 2022, where he briefly references Marcos Nobres' analysis of the Bolsonaro government. The article and interview can be found using the following links:
www1.folha.uol.com.br/ilustrissima/2020/01/alvim-errou-a-mao-na-trollagem-bolsonarista-inspirada-na-direita-dos-eua.shtml;
www.ihu.unisinos.br/159-noticias/entrevistas/608123-bolsonarismo-como-identidade-coletiva-a-logica-sacrificial-e-a-brutalizacao-dos-afetos-entrevista-especial-com-rodrigo-nunes.

17 *Troll, trollar, trollagem* are popular expressions that have been circulating for decades in the gay world in Brazil, to refer to quests in search of romantic and sexual partners. These terms were incorporated into the language of digital culture in the 1990s, to designate systematic provocateurs active online, whose fallacies, disturbing interventions, and redirectioning of discussions tend to cause indignation, multidirectional engagement, and bellicose interactions.

18 Nuno Ramos, "O baile da ilha fiscal," *Folha de São Paulo* (May 3, 2020): www1.folha.uol.com.br/ilustrissima/2020/05/brasil-enfrenta-duplo-apocalipse-com-bolsonaro-e-coronavirus-reflete-nuno-ramos.shtml.

19 Ibid.

20 Luiz Eduardo Soares, *Dentro da noite feroz: o fascismo no Brasil* (São Paulo: Boitempo, 2020): 71–2.

21 Some expressions activated by reactionary Brazilian linguistic practices and converted into socially active stereotypes with the political rise of far-right extremist movements were fundamental in constructing targets for coordinated harassment and hate speech. Examples of these targets include independent women, homosexuals, journalists, intellectual workers, scientists, artists, and professors.
22 Victor Klemperer, *Language of the Third Reich*, trans. Martin Brady (London: Bloomsbury Academic, 2013): 29.
23 Julián Fuks, *A ocupação* (São Paulo: Companhia das Letras): 7.
24 Noemi Jaffe, *O que ela sussurra* (São Paulo: Companhia das Letras, 2020).
25 Silviano Santiago, "Ovos de marimbondo, uma fábula" (2020). See https://pernambucorevista.com.br/acervo/pernambuco/2522-ovos-de-marimbondo,-uma-f%C3%A1bula.html.
26 This quote is extracted from a comment by Jean-Pierre Sarrazac on Brecht's concept of fabulation. See Sarrazac, *O futuro do drama* (Porto: Campo das Letras, 2002): 34.
27 Santiago, "Ovos."
28 Ibid.
29 Ibid.
30 Renata Mariz, "Número de brasileiros que se tornam atiradores para obter licença explode no país," *O Globo* (July 30, 2017): https://oglobo.globo.com/politica/numero-de-brasileiros-que-se-tornam-atiradores-para-obter-licenca-explode-no-pais-21645849.
31 See the following two interviews by Lenora de Barros, among others: https://artebrasileiros.com.br/arte/lenora-de-barros-enfrenta-o-medo and www1.folha.uol.com.br/ilustrada/2017/11/1937117-lenora-de-barros-aposta-na-ceramica-em-nova-exposicao-no-anexo-millan.shtml.
32 Catherine Craft, *Jasper Johns* (New York: Parkstone Press, 2009): 35–6.
33 Nuno Ramos, *Fooquedeu (Um diário)* (São Paulo: Ed. Todavia, 2022): 192.
34 Samuel Beckett, *Company* (London: Marion Boyars, 1996).
35 Grace Passô, *Vaga carne* (Belo Horizonte: Editora Javali, 2018): 15.
36 Ibid.
37 Maria Caroline, "Manifestações: o teatro e o Brasil, por Grace Passô (atriz e dramaturga)": http://df.divirtasemais.com.br/app/noticia/programe-se/2013/06/21/noticia_programese,142510/veja-comentario-da-atriz-e-dramaturga-grace-passo-sobre-o-teatro-e-o-b.shtml.
38 Ibid.
39 For more on *Lígia*, see the artist's website: www.nunoramos.com.br/trabalhos/ligia.
40 Nuno Ramos, "JN, 16.3.2016," in *Fooquedeu*, 38–9.

41 Ibid.
42 Ibid.
43 Jaffe, *O que ela sussurra*.
44 Ibid.
45 Ibid.
46 Part of the video can be seen at: www.desvirtual.com/project/odiolandia-hateland.
47 The Rádio USP broadcast and a list of the related commentaries can be accessed here: www.desvirtual.com/grupos-de-odio-contra-os-sem-teto.
48 Following are some examples of the phrases compiled by Beiguelman: *Lugar de bandido é na vala. Já foi tarde. – Invasor é pior que erva daninha, por onde passa deixa sua marca. – Morte de político é limpeza no país – Pena que deu tempo de saírem ... – Tá achando ruim? Abre as portas da tua casa para os sem teto morar então. – Queria ver a cara dela agora, derretendo no inferno. – Seria melhor se estivesse cheio de venezuelanos, haitianos, bolivianos. – Sejamos sensatos, tem que matar, senão não resolve. – Que coisa linda. Deixa a gente aqui do interior fazer isso com os sem-terra, mas usando a 12 com chumbo 3T.*
49 Beiguelman, cited in Leila Kiyomura, "Cracolândia é destaque na 1ª Bienal de Arte Digital" *Jornal da USP* (April 17, 2018): https://jornal.usp.br/cultura/cracolandia-e-destaque-na-1a-bienal-de-arte-digital.
50 The vote that initiated impeachment proceedings against President Dilma Rousseff took place on April 17, 2016. *Abril* incorporates fragments of the speeches made during the final vote of Rousseff's impeachment process. It was directed by Eryk Rocha and Gabriela Carneiro da Cunha, written by Eryk Rocha, Gabriela Carneiro da Cunha, Carolina Virguez, Julia Ariani, and Bruno Carneiro, in collaboration with "os dramaturgos da farsa de todos os dias"; with a performance by Carolina Virguez. The synopsis reads: "To bring to a stop the state of being closed off; To bring to a stop the state of inactivity of certain things; To disunite, to elongate; To make it function or circulate; To uncover; To unwrap or tear apart; To dig up so it gets deeper; To make accessible; To begin to; To give an opportunity to; To open. It opened. Access. Abril. A scenic dialogue between theater and genre cinema where through the television frame a woman sees a world of horror. New and old ghosts same old ghosts once again haunt the month of April." Translation by Flora Süssekind.
51 Giselle Beiguelman. *Odiolândia* (São Paulo: N-1 Edições, 2018): 9.
52 The motet can be accessed at: www.youtube.com/watch?v=GIaMUmJNNWc.
53 Lima Barreto, *Sátiras e outras subversões: textos inéditos*, ed. Felipe Botelho Corrêa (São Paulo: Companhia das Letras, 2016).

54 Ibid., 13.
55 Lima Barreto, *Antologia de artigos, cartas e crônicas sobre trabalhadores*, ed. Antônio Augusto Moreira de Faria and Rosalvo Gonçalves Pinto (Belo Horizonte: FALE/UFMG, 2012): 41.
56 Ibid., 60.
57 *Cartas ao mundo* (2022) is a documentary-manifesto by Bia Lessa, in film-triptych format featuring three episodes/films: *Asfixia*, *Mercadoria*, and *O comum*. Approximate length of each film is 50 minutes. All three episodes are available on the streaming channels for Curta and Globoplay, and on Canal Inhotim's YouTube page: https://youtube.com/playlist?list=PLZi10Sa5oRtGCHVRuyi4WVCPP7F31Gzct&si=xqJcnQ2AP1_smgYU.
58 A version of *A gente se vê por aqui* was presented during the 31st Festival de Arte de Porto Alegre in 2017. Another version was shown at the 5th Mostra Internacional de Teatro in São Paulo in 2018.
59 *Aos vivos: Debates* is a series of three plays produced on the respective dates of the three presidential debates that took place in 2018: *Debate n.1 – Dervixe*, *Debate n.2 – Antígona*, and *Debate n.3 – Terra em Transe*. As is well known, only the first play reproduced, simultaneously, the debate between the candidates. The other two debates were cancelled after the stabbing of Jair Bolsonaro, which justified Bolsonaro's absence from these debates.
60 *Dito e feito*, performance produced between June 15 and June 18, 2021, at the Instituto Ling in Porto Alegre.
61 On the Wooster Group, see https://thewoostergroup.org/blog.
62 Ricardo Aleixo, *Extraquadro* (Belo Horizonte: Impressões de Minas, 2021).
63 Ibid., 21.
64 Ibid., 41–5.
65 "rumor / das imagens / umas contra / as outras / umas rentes / às outras / umas dentro /das outras / umas."

Index

Entries in italics indicate a page with an illustration.